# Practice Tests

Lori Riverstone-Newell
*Illinois State University*

# American Government

Twelfth Edition

## Walter E. Volkomer
*Hunter College of the City University of New York*

PEARSON

Prentice
Hall

PRENTICE HALL, Upper Saddle River, NJ 07458

Copyright © 2008 by Pearson Education, Inc.
Upper Saddle River, New Jersey 07458
All right reserved

Printed in the United States
10 9 8 7 6 5 4 3 2 1

ISBN 10: 0-13-236458-1
ISBN 13: 978-0-13-236458-4

# CONTENTS

Preface to the Student                                                    iv

Chapter 1     Politics, Democracy, and the American People          1

Chapter 2     From Colonialism to Constitutionalism                7

Chapter 3     The Federal System                                   14

Chapter 4     Public Opinion and the Mass Media                    23

Chapter 5     Political Parties and Interest Groups                32

Chapter 6     Nominations and Elections                            40

Chapter 7     Congress                                             49

Chapter 8     The Chief Executive                                  59

Chapter 9     The Federal Bureaucracy                              66

Chapter 10    The Judiciary                                        74

Chapter 11    Civil Liberties                                      82

Chapter 12    Civil Rights                                         95

Chapter 13    Public Policy—What Government Does                  103

Chapter 14    Foreign Policy                                      111

Answer Key                                                        121

# PREFACE TO THE STUDENT

The material in this booklet is designed to identify the key points in the corresponding *American Government* text and to promote your understanding of the government and political system of the United States.

Each chapter begins with a brief overview of the material covered in the corresponding chapter of your textbook, *American Government*. A series of learning objectives is then identified, followed by an outline of the chapter, a summary of the chapter, and a list of key terms covered in the chapter. Each chapter concludes with a series of practice exercises that provide an opportunity for you to assess your understanding and mastery of the material covered in the chapter. The final exercise relates to the ABC News/Prentice Hall Video Library DVDs that are included with your textbook.

Before reading each chapter in the *American Government* text, review the Chapter Overview, Learning Objectives, and Chapter Outline sections of this booklet. After you have read a chapter in the text, read the Chapter Summary and Key Terms section of this booklet to review the material from the text. Use the Practice Exercises, in conjunction with the Answer Key provided at the end of this booklet, to assess your comprehension of the text material, and review material as appropriate. Finally, view the video clips on the ABC News/Prentice Hall Video Library DVDs and try to answer the Critical Thinking Questions that follow each program summary (these are open-ended questions and the answers are not included in the Answer Key).

The political system and politics of the United States have implications for citizens and politics worldwide. This booklet is designed to help you better understand the government and politics of this influential nation.

# CHAPTER 1
## POLITICS, DEMOCRACY, AND THE AMERICAN PEOPLE

## CHAPTER OVERVIEW

Chapter 1 of *American Government* explores the nature of politics and political power, distinguishes between government and politics, and develops the concepts of power, politics, legitimacy, and government. The chapter discusses the meaning of democracy and the distinction between representative and direct democracy.

The chapter then develops principles associated with democracy, including self-government, the social contract, majority rule, and minority rights. The chapter stresses the significance of limited government and constitutional democracy in the United States, reflecting the importance of placing limits on the authority of government.

Chapter 1 concludes with a discussion of democracy and diversity, including a review of the significant demographic trends in the U.S. population.

## LEARNING OBJECTIVES

1.  Define politics, political power, and government and assess the relationships among the three concepts.
2.  Outline the sources of a government's legitimacy.
3.  Compare and contrast direct and representative forms of democracy.
4.  Define referendum, initiative, and recall.
5.  Explain the contributions of John Locke, Baron Montesquieu, and James Madison to the philosophical principles of American government.
6.  Outline the fundamental principles of American government.
7.  Discuss the problems and contributions of diversity in a democratic society.

## CHAPTER OUTLINE

I.   The nature of politics
     A. Politics and power
     B. The bases of political power
         1. Tradition
         2. Charisma
         3. Legality
     C. Politics and government
         1. Difference between politics and government
         2. Government for all members of society
II.  The meaning of democracy
     A. The bases of democracy
         1. Self-government
         2. The social contract

       3. Majority rule
       4. Minority rights
       5. Limited government
       6. Democratic institutions
       7. Free elections
       8. An organized opposition
       9. Free expression of ideas
      10. Equality
      11. Universal education
III.    Democracy and diversity
     A. Trends in the U.S. population
     B. The influence of diversity on politics

## CHAPTER SUMMARY

Politics is the process of deciding who gets what in a society. Political scientists study politics that affect large numbers of people and involve significant amounts of political power. Political power is the ability to influence the political behavior of others. A political official can exercise power only if the public acknowledges that power as legitimate and believes that the rules and decisions stemming from it are proper.

Democracy is a form of government in which policy decisions are based on the consent of the governed and citizens are guaranteed certain basic rights. For the most part, democracy in the United States is representative democracy rather than direct democracy. The processes of referendum, initiative, and recall are examples of direct democracy that exist in some states and localities in the United States.

The guiding principles of democracy in the United States include self-government, the social contract, majority rule, minority rights, limited government, free expression, free elections, and universal education. Democratic principles include the right of each person to have equality before the law, equality of political rights, and equality of economic and social opportunity.

The U.S. population has grown significantly over time and is becoming increasingly diverse. Diversity creates special problems for a democracy, because it leads to wide differences of opinion and increases the difficulty of reaching an agreement on solutions to political problems. Managing a democracy as large and diverse as the U.S. democracy is a great challenge.

## KEY TERMS

civil liberties

constitutional democracy

democracy

direct democracy

government

legitimacy

majority rule

minority rights

political parties

political power

politics

representative democracy

self-government

social contract

# PRACTICE EXERCISES

## FILL IN THE BLANKS

1. _____ is the process of deciding who gets what in a society.

2. If people accept the rules and decisions made by a political official as right and proper, the political power exercised by that official may be described as _____.

3. According to Max Weber, legitimacy in politics is based on three sources: _____, _____, and _____.

4. The term _____ refers to the institutions and processes by which societal rules are made and enforced.

5. Democracy in the United States is primarily _____ democracy.

6. The _____ system allows citizens to place a proposal on a ballot by obtaining a required number of signatures.

7. In the view of British philosopher John Locke, a(n) _____ is an agreement among members of a society to accept existing laws and penalties as binding.

8. According to Thomas Jefferson, majority rule is legitimate only if it respects and protects _____ rights.

9. The U.S. Constitution set up a government with three branches: _____, _____, and _____.

10. In 2006, the Census Bureau reported that 12.6 percent of the U.S. population lives below the official _____ line.

## MULTIPLE CHOICE

11. Harold Lasswell has defined politics as
    a. the actions of political parties.
    b. constitutionalism.
    c. representative democracy.
    d. the study of who gets what, when, and how.

12. When citizens vote directly for or against the adoption of a particular law, they are participating in
    a. representative democracy.
    b. republican government.
    c. a referendum.
    d. a recall.

13. The American two-party system is an example of what source of political legitimacy?
   a. rules
   b. legal
   c. charismatic
   d. traditional

14. The importance of charisma as a source of political legitimacy reflects an emphasis on
   a. law.
   b. tradition.
   c. rules.
   d. personality.

15. In a town meeting, citizens gather to make decisions for their community. This is a form of
   a. direct democracy.
   b. representative democracy.
   c. constitutional democracy.
   d. unicameral democracy.

16. In John Locke's view, natural rights
   a. exist independent of society and government, and government exists to protect these rights.
   b. are those rights that are granted by a nation's constitution.
   c. are subject to determination by government.
   d. are derived from the social contract.

17. Voters may vote on whether an elected official may continue to hold office in the process of
   a. recall.
   b. majority rule.
   c. initiative.
   d. referendum.

18. In his book on the operation of democracy in the United States, Alexis de Tocqueville warned against
   a. the social contract.
   b. natural law.
   c. the tyranny of the majority.
   d. the tyranny of the minority.

19. The preservation of minority rights involves
   a. majority acceptance of the policies preferred by the minority.
   b. minority acceptance of the policies preferred by the majority.
   c. allowing the minority to violate the rights of the majority.
   d. granting certain basic freedoms to the minority.

20. The rights protected in the first ten amendments to the Constitution are usually referred to as
   a. natural law.
   b. minority rights.
   c. freedom of expression.
   d. civil liberties.

21. The U.S. Constitution is an attempt to put into practice the ideas of
   a. majority government.
   b. limited government, constitutionalism, and minority rights.
   c. natural law and representation.
   d. minority rule and majority rights.

22. The political philosopher who argued in support of separation of the basic functions of government was
   a. Aristotle.
   b. Plato.
   c. Machiavelli.
   d. Montesquieu.

23. An important aspect of the American electoral system is
   a. the requirement to vote.
   b. an organized opposition.
   c. the secret ballot.
   d. freedom of speech.

24. Historically, equality as a democratic value has meant
   a. economic equality.
   b. political and legal equality.
   c. choosing equality at the expense of liberty.
   d. choosing economic equality over political equality.

25. Eighteen-year-olds were first allowed to vote in
   a. the first presidential election following adoption of the Constitution.
   b. the 1820s.
   c. the 1920s.
   d. the 1970s.

TRUE OR FALSE

26. The men who drafted the U.S. Constitution were not overly optimistic about human nature.
   T   F

27. In a representative democracy, each voter is able to participate directly in the decision-making process.
   T   F

28. A referendum is an example of direct democracy.
T  F

29. All constitutional democracies are characterized by the division of government into three branches: executive, legislative, and judicial.
T  F

30. Democracy as it was practiced in ancient Athens is remarkably similar to democracy as it exists today in the United States.
T  F


## DISCUSSION, ESSAY

31. Identify and discuss the extent to which the American political system is viewed with cynicism. What are the sources of this cynicism, and to what extent is the cynicism warranted?

32. Identify and describe examples of political legitimacy derived from each of Weber's three sources: tradition, charisma, and legality.

33. Distinguish between representative and direct democracy, and discuss the strengths and weaknesses associated with each.

34. Identify and describe the principles that form the basis for democracy in the United States.

35. Describe some ways in which the population of the United States is changing, and explain why the growing diversity may create special problems.

# CHAPTER 2
## FROM COLONIALISM TO CONSTITUTIONALISM

### CHAPTER OVERVIEW

Chapter 2 begins by reviewing the events leading to the end of the colonial era and the process by which the Articles of Confederation were ratified by the Continental Congress. It examines the strengths and weaknesses of government under the Articles of Confederation and discusses developments leading to the Constitutional Convention of 1787.

The chapter describes key issues that were debated at the Constitutional Convention and how these issues were resolved in the writing of the Constitution. The chapter identifies the fundamental ideas that motivated the delegates to the Constitutional Convention and the devices incorporated in the design of the U.S. government to restrain the power of the central government, including federalism and separation of powers.

The chapter concludes with a discussion of constitutional amendments and a brief consideration of the roles of experience, accepted practice, and judicial interpretation in the development of the U.S. political system.

### LEARNING OBJECTIVES

1.  Assess the influence English legal and political traditions had upon the framers of the U.S. Constitution.
2.  Outline the early attempts of the colonists to form a national government.
3.  Describe the symbolic and political significance of the Declaration of Independence.
4.  Explain the basic features of the Articles of Confederation.
5.  Compare and contrast the Articles of Confederation and the U.S. Constitution.
6.  Assess the issues which divided delegates to the Philadelphia Constitutional Convention, and the mechanisms by which those differences were resolved.
7.  Define the philosophical differences between the Federalists and the Antifederalists.
8.  Outline the fundamental principles of the Constitution which emerged from the Constitutional Convention.
9.  Explain the formal and informal methods of amending the Constitution.

### CHAPTER OUTLINE

I.  The road to independence
    A. Early attempts at cooperation
    B. The First Continental Congress
    C. The revolution
    D. The Declaration of Independence
II. The Articles of Confederation
    A. Government under the Articles
    B. Problems under the Articles

III.    The Constitutional Convention
        A. The delegates
        B. The issues
            1. A national government versus states' rights
            2. Large states versus small states
            3. North versus South
            4. Selecting government officials
        C. Ratification
            1. The demand for a Bill of Rights
            2. The Federalist Papers
IV.     The U.S. Constitution
        A. Federalism
        B. Separation of powers
        C. Checks and balances: Shared powers
            1. Impeachment
            2. Bicameral legislature
            3. Selection of public officials
        D. Judicial review
        E. Popular sovereignty
        F. National supremacy
V.      Constitutional change and development
        A. Amending the Constitution
        B. Other means of constitutional development


CHAPTER SUMMARY


The process of political independence for the American colonies began with early attempts at cooperation among the colonists. Rising dissatisfaction with British policies led to the meeting of the First Continental Congress in 1774.

The Declaration of Independence was adopted by the Continental Congress on July 4, 1776, and announced that the American states were free from British rule. It was not until 1781, when the Articles of Confederation were ratified, that a central government was established among the states. The new government had very little power; it could neither tax individuals nor regulate commerce. Problems under the Articles of Confederation, as evidenced by incidents such as Shays's Rebellion, led to calls for revision of the Articles and what would become the Constitutional Convention.

In 1787, the Constitutional Convention approved the U.S. Constitution. The delegates to the convention dealt with issues including nationalism versus states' rights, large states versus small states, and North versus South. The delegates wanted to create a central government with adequate powers, but they also wanted to restrain those powers.

The Constitution is based on several key concepts, including federalism, separation of powers, checks and balances, judicial review, popular sovereignty, and national supremacy. It has been amended 27 times. The first 10 Amendments to the Constitution, known as the Bill of Rights, protects individuals against the power of central government. They were ratified in 1791.

The Constitution provides a written outline for the United States political system. However, some aspects of the political system are not found in the words of the Constitution. For instance, there is no mention in the Constitution of political parties or the cabinet. These are examples of how the political system has developed from experience and accepted practice.

## KEY TERMS

amendment
Antifederalists
Articles of Confederation
bicameral legislature
bill of rights
checks and balances
Connecticut Compromise
Constitutional Convention
Electoral College
English Bill of Rights
federalism
Federalists

First Continental Congress
impeachment
judicial review
Magna Carta
national supremacy
New Jersey Plan
popular sovereignty
ratification
Second Continental Congress
separation of powers
Shays's Rebellion
state sovereignty
Virginia Plan

## PRACTICE EXERCISES

### FILL IN THE BLANKS

1.  When American colonists rebelled against English rule and demanded their rights, they were demanding the rights of _____ citizens.

2.  The first document that provided a framework of government for the American states was the _____ _____ _____.

3.  The 1786 Massachusetts uprising against state courts because of mortgage foreclosures on farms is known as _____ _____.

4.  Under the ____ ____ ____, a legislature would be created with each state having the same number of representatives regardless of its population.

5.  As specified in the Constitution, the president is indirectly selected by the _____ _____.

6.  In the debate over ratification of the Constitution, supporters of the Constitution were called _____.

7.  In a federal system, the _____ level of government has authority over the entire territory.

8.  The power of courts to declare legislative and executive actions of government unconstitutional is called _____ _____.

9.  The idea that people are the source of all legal authority is known as _____ _____.

10. The series of 85 essays that were written in support of the U.S. Constitution and published in New York newspapers are collectively known as the _____ _____.

MULTIPLE CHOICE

11. The colonists denounced English laws such as the Sugar Act because
    a. they believed they violated the fundamental English right that guaranteed that taxes could only be imposed by elected representatives.
    b. they did not believe that Parliament had the right to make any laws for the colonists.
    c. it was in violation of the Albany Plan.
    d. it was in violation of the Quartering Act.

12. What was the main purpose of the "committees of correspondence"?
    a. to establish a communication network between colonies
    b. to plan secret attacks on British soldiers
    c. to organize the first battles of the revolution
    d. to give a forum for colonists to voice dissent

13. According to the text, which of the following documents is credited with turning the tide of public opinion in favor of a formal break with England?
    a. *The Federalist Papers*
    b. Declaration of Independence
    c. Thomas Paine's *Common Sense*
    d. Articles of Confederation

14. The Federalists and Antifederalists tended to differ in that
    a. Federalists came from more populous states.
    b. Federalists were more likely to be farmers.
    c. leading Federalists were an average of ten to twelve years younger than prominent Antifederalists.
    d. Federalists were more likely to have begun their careers in service to the state governments.

15. The compromise adopted by the Constitutional Convention which permitted slave-holding states to partially count slaves so as to increase representation in the House of Representatives was the
    a. commerce compromise.
    b. three-fifths rule.
    c. treaty ratification compromise.
    d. supremacy clause.

16. Under the New Jersey Plan, which preserved the basic elements of the confederate system,
    a. the national legislature would be bicameral.
    b. the number of representatives in the national legislature would be determined by population.
    c. each state would be represented equally in a unicameral legislature.
    d. Congress would have the power to impose duties on foreign goods without the approval of the states.

17. Which of the following statements summarizes the Connecticut Compromise?
    a. The national legislature would be unicameral.
    b. The national legislature would be bicameral.
    c. In the House of Representatives, each state would have equal representation.
    d. In the Senate, representation would be based on population.

18. Under the Electoral College system, each state chooses
    a. two electors.
    b. one elector.
    c. a number of electors equal to the number of the state's representatives in Congress.
    d. a number of electors equal to the combined number of the state's senators and representatives in Congress.

19. Federalism serves the basic purpose of limiting the power of government
    a. by dividing power along geographic lines.
    b. by providing for popular sovereignty.
    c. by providing for judicial review.
    d. by dividing power among the executive, legislative, and judicial branches.

20. The president nominates Supreme Court justices, but the Senate must confirm justices. This illustrates the principle of
    a. national supremacy.
    b. judicial review.
    c. checks and balances.
    d. separation of powers.

21. The Constitution gives the sole power of impeachment to
    a. the president.
    b. the Supreme Court.
    c. the House.
    d. the Senate.

22. Following impeachment, an official is removed from office only if
    a. a majority of the Supreme Court vote in favor of removal from office.
    b. a majority of the Senate vote in favor of removal from office.
    c. a majority of the House vote in favor of removal from office.
    d. two-thirds of the Senate vote in favor of removal from office.

23. Which federal official has the longest term of office?
    a. representative
    b. president
    c. senator
    d. federal judge

24. The Supreme Court case of *Marbury* v. *Madison* established the principle of
   a. judicial review.
   b. federalism.
   c. popular sovereignty.
   d. national supremacy.

25. The Federalist party was led by
   a. Thomas Paine and Thomas Jefferson.
   b. Alexander Hamilton and John Adams.
   c. George Washington and Thomas Jefferson.
   d. Samuel Adams and James Madison.

## TRUE OR FALSE

26. The delegates to the Constitutional Convention of 1787 represented the diversity of the colonial population, including women and laborers.
   T  F

27. An important weakness of the Articles of Confederation was the provision of too little authority for the central government to tax or regulate commerce.
   T  F

28. The Virginia Plan called for a unicameral legislature, with each state having equal representation.
   T  F

29. The Articles of Confederation were based on a theory of state sovereignty.
   T  F

30. The Supreme Court's power of judicial review extends not only to actions of the president and Congress but also to actions of state governments.
   T  F

## DISCUSSION, ESSAY

31. On what basis did the American colonists rebel against British rule?  Explain whether the colonists were demanding rights different from those of British citizens.

32. Identify the weaknesses of the Articles of Confederation and discuss how these weaknesses were addressed by the Constitution.

33. Discuss how the Federalists and Antifederalists differed from each other, and explain their arguments for and against the Constitution.

34. Identify some of the amendments to the Constitution, and discuss the types of amendments that are more or less likely to be seriously debated and considered for adoption.

35. Identify and discuss some of the important elements of the political system that are not specifically mentioned in the Constitution. Discuss whether and why the authors of the Constitution would likely view these as favorable or unfavorable developments.

# CHAPTER 3
# THE FEDERAL SYSTEM

## CHAPTER OVERVIEW

Chapter 3 describes the federal form of government created by the U.S. Constitution, and identifies the powers of the national and state governments, as well as the limitations on these powers. The chapter discusses the historical development of relations between the federal and state governments, identifies how historical conflicts over slavery and the New Deal illustrate differing views of federalism, and describes how the U.S. system of federalism has changed over time.

The chapter concludes with a consideration of Supreme Court cases that reveal a continuing change in the relationship and distribution of power between the federal and state governments.

## LEARNING OBJECTIVES

1. Compare and contrast the three different models for organizing relations between a central government and constituent governments.
2. Identify and discuss the classification of powers between national and state governments.
3. Assess the constitutional relationship between the states.
4. Explain the significance of the case of *McCulloch* v. *Maryland (1819)* in the evolution of American federalism.
5. Explain the importance of the Ninth and Tenth Amendments of the U.S. Constitution in the context of American federalism.
6. Trace the evolution of the nation-state relationship under American federalism as it pertains to the sharing of governing power.
7. Identify the mechanisms by which the national government may exercise control over state governments in particular issue areas.
8. Define "Full Faith and Credit" and explain the concept's importance to federal systems.

## CHAPTER OUTLINE

I. Federalism in the Constitution
   A. Powers of the national government
      1. Delegated powers
      2. Implied powers
   B. Limitations on the national government
      1. Prohibitions on bills of attainder
      2. Prohibitions on *ex post facto* laws
      3. Limits on power to suspend writs of *habeas corpus*
      4. Constitutional guarantees of the Bill of Rights

C. Reserved Powers of the states
    1. Reserved powers
D. Concurrent powers
    1. Tax and spend
    2. Borrow money
    3. Exercise eminent domain
    4. Establish courts
    5. Enforce laws
E. Limitations on the states
    1. Article I, Section 10
    2. Constitutional amendments
F. Interstate relations
    1. Full faith and credit clause
    2. Debate over same-sex marriage
    3. Privileges and immunities clause
    4. Interstate rendition clause
    5. Interstate compacts
    6. U.S. Supreme Court original jurisdiction

II.   Mutual obligations of the national and state governments
A. National supremacy
    1. Constitutional requirement of Article VI of the Constitution
    2. U.S. Supreme Court as arbiter of the Constitution

III.  Federalism in theory and practice
A. The growth of the grant system
B. Centralized federalism
C. The New Federalism
    1. Nixon's New Federalism
        a. General revenue sharing
        b. Block grants
    2. Reagan's New Federalism
        a. Increased use of block grants
        b. Goal of elimination of many federal aid plans
    3. Welfare reform
    4. War on terrorism
        a. USA PATRIOT Act
        b. Budgetary concerns
    5. Future trends in the federal system

IV.  The Supreme Court and modern federalism
A. Changing the restricted view of the power of congress
    1. Roosevelt's "court packing plan"
    2. Invalidating federal laws
    3. Restricting the forms of federal authority
B. The future path of the Supreme Court

# CHAPTER SUMMARY

The Constitution creates a federal form of government, wherein neither the federal government nor the states have absolute power. Decisions and functions are divided between the two levels of government.

The Constitution delegates specific powers to the national government. These powers include the authority to regulate interstate commerce and the powers to declare war and negotiate treaties with other nations. In addition, the Constitution gives Congress implied powers under the necessary and proper clause.

Some powers, called concurrent powers, are shared between the federal and state governments. Examples of concurrent powers are the powers to tax and borrow money. The Tenth Amendment makes clear that all powers not delegated to the federal government are reserved to the states. Education and police protection are two examples of reserved powers.

Constitutional obligations of the federal government to the states include the guarantee clause, and the requirement that the federal government protect the states against foreign invasion or internal violence. Constitutional obligations of the states to the federal government include that the states abide by the supremacy clause. Also, the role of the federal government vis-à-vis the states has dramatically changed after the September 11 attacks, and the continuing war against terrorism.

The Constitution limits the power of both the national and state governments and defines rules which govern interstate relations such as the full faith and credit clause. Recently this clause has been the source of controversy in regard to the legality of same-sex marriage in the state of Massachusetts and the legalization of marijuana for medicinal purposes.

From its earliest years, the nation has witnessed an ongoing debate between supporters of a strong national government and supporters of stronger state governments. Arguments surrounding the Civil War and the New Deal illustrate distinct views of federalism, and the outcomes of both the Civil War and the New Deal have greatly changed the nature of federalism in the United States. As the influence of the federal government has increased over time, attempts have been made to return some power to the states in a process referred to as devolution.

The Supreme Court has played an important role in the history of federalism, and the future of federalism will be influenced by future Supreme Court decisions in this area. Since 1995, the Supreme Court has moved in some cases to impose restrictions on the federal government's power over the states. It is too soon to say whether these Supreme Court decisions are the beginning of a fundamental shift in federalism that would return greater power to the states. This is illustrated by a recent ruling asserting the sovereign immunity of states from both private lawsuits brought in federal court and from administrative claims brought before federal agencies.

# KEY TERMS

bills of attainder
block grant
centralized federalism
concurrent powers
confederation
cooperative federalism
delegated powers
due process clause
equal protection clause
*ex post facto* laws
federalism
full faith and credit clause
grant-in-aid

guarantee clause
implied powers
interstate compacts
interstate rendition clause
necessary and proper clause
original jurisdiction
privileges and immunities clause
reserved powers
unitary government
writ of *habeas corpus*

# PRACTICE EXERCISES

## FILL IN THE BLANKS

1. A government where the powers of the central government are granted by state or provincial governments is called a _____.

2. The Constitution gives two basic types of powers to the national government: _____ powers and _____ powers.

3. Powers shared by both the federal and state governments are called concurrent powers. The powers of the states under the Constitution are referred to as _____ powers.

4. The powers given to Congress by Article I, Section 8, of the Constitution "to make all laws which shall be necessary and proper" to carry out the powers expressly granted by the Constitution are called _____ powers.

5. States are required to honor the civil rulings of other states under the _____ _____ _____ _____clause.

6. The Constitution gives the right to create and administer a public school system to the _____ level of government.

7. The Constitution permits the _____ _____ to settle disputes between two or more states.

8. The constitutional statement that the United States shall ensure states a republican form of government is referred to as the _____ clause.

9. A sum of money that is given by the national government to a state to be used for a broad, general purpose is called a _____ grant.

10. The term _____ Federalism has been used to describe the approach to federalism adopted by Republican presidents since the late 1960s, including Presidents Nixon and Reagan.


MULTIPLE CHOICE

11. A government in which the central government has ultimate legal authority over its citizens is called a
   a. confederation.
   b. monarchy.
   c. unitary government.
   d. constitutional government.

12. Which of the following countries is an example of a confederate government?
   a. United States
   b. Israel
   c. United Kingdom
   d. Switzerland

13. The power to regulate interstate commerce is an example of
   a. an implied power.
   b. a reserved power.
   c. a prohibited power.
   d. a delegated power.

14. Which of the following clauses from the Constitution did the Civil Rights Act of 1964 use to outlaw racial discrimination in hotels, motels, and many restaurants?
   a. the interstate rendition clause
   b. the full faith and credit clause
   c. the commerce clause
   d. the privileges and immunities clause

15. The Supreme Court case of *McCulloch* v. *Maryland* set the precedent for
   a. judicial review.
   b. a broad interpretation of the implied powers of Congress.
   c. freedom of religion.
   d. strict federal enforcement of election laws.

16. The reserved powers of the states under the U.S. Constitution are identified in which part of the Constitution?
   a. Article I
   b. Article II
   c. the First Amendment
   d. the Tenth Amendment

17. Which of the following is NOT a concurrent power?
    a. power to borrow money
    b. power to enforce the laws
    c. power to tax and spend
    d. power to regulate interstate commerce

18. Legislative acts that single out certain people for punishment without trial are called
    a. bills of attainder.
    b. *ex post facto* laws.
    c. due process.
    d. equal protection.

19. The constitutional clause that mandates that a state return a person charged with a crime in another state to the state where the crime was committed is the
    a. privileges and immunities clause.
    b. interstate rendition clause.
    c. full faith and credit clause.
    d. due process clause.

20. The congressional act passed in 1996 asserting that no state will be required to recognize any same-sex marriage that is granted under the law of another state is called the
    a. privileges and immunities clause.
    b. interstate rendition clause.
    c. Civil Rights Act.
    d. Defense of Marriage Act.

21. The creation of the Port Authority of New York and New Jersey in 1921 had constitutional grounding based on the
    a. privileges and immunities clause.
    b. interstate rendition clause.
    c. Fourteenth Amendment.
    d. ability of states to enter into interstate compacts.

22. In the dispute over slavery, defenders of slavery argued that the national government had no authority to interfere with the system because
    a. the Constitution explicitly permitted slavery.
    b. the Constitution was silent on the legal status of slavery.
    c. the Constitution did not give states the right to secede from the Union.
    d. the Constitution had been created by the states, and the states could withdraw from the Union if the national government violated the rights of the states.

23. The program under which the national government gained vast new power to regulate the economy and social welfare programs such as Social Security was
    a. the New Deal.
    b. centralized federalism.
    c. state-centered federalism.
    d. the New Federalism.

24. Welfare reform under the Personal Responsibility and Work Opportunity Reconciliation Act of 1996 is an example of
   a. the New Deal.
   b. centralized federalism.
   c. state-centered federalism.
   d. the New Federalism.

25. The Supreme Court decision in *United States* v. *Lopez*, which declared unconstitutional a statute that made it a federal crime to possess a weapon within 1000 feet of a school building, was significant because
   a. it reaffirmed the trend toward centralization of government power.
   b. it signaled a shift in the Supreme Court's willingness to reject constitutional challenges to congressional legislation based on the commerce clause.
   c. it found parts of the New Deal to be unconstitutional.
   d. it found parts of the Civil Rights Act of 1964 to be unconstitutional.

TRUE OR FALSE

26. Confederate governments are relatively rare.
   T  F

27. The power to conduct foreign affairs rests exclusively with the federal government.
   T  F

28. Reserved powers refer to those shared by the state and national governments.
   T  F

29. The U.S. Supreme Court often hears cases based on its original jurisdiction in conflicts between the states.
   T  F

30. Recent Supreme Court decisions concerning federalism clearly support the trend toward centralization of governmental authority that has existed since the 1930s.
   T  F

DISCUSSION, ESSAY

31. Compare and contrast the strengths and weaknesses of unitary, federal, and confederate forms of government.

32. Distinguish among delegated, concurrent, and reserved powers in the federal system, and provide examples of each.

33. What are the constitutional limitations on the state and federal governments?

34. Identify and discuss the conditions under which the federal government has the right to intervene in a state with federal troops or by calling the state militia into federal service. Identify historical examples of such federal intervention in the states, and discuss whether these interventions should have occurred.

35. Identify important developments in the history of U.S. federalism, and discuss how and why the relationship between the federal and state governments is likely to change in the future. Be sure to explain the impact of the September 11 attacks upon future patterns of federalism.

## ABC NEWS/PRENTICE HALL VIDEO LIBRARY: AMERICAN GOVERNMENT

### MOMENT OF CRISIS—SYSTEM FAILURE
**Originally Aired: 9/15/05**
**Program: *Primetime***
**Running Time: 29:12**

Katrina ranks as the country's most expensive natural disaster and one of the deadliest in U.S. history. It has killed more than 700 people, uprooted tens of thousands of families, destroyed countless homes, and forced the evacuation of a major American city. Two and a half weeks after the hurricane roared ashore, just east of New Orleans, the country is trying to make sense of the resulting failures of local, state, and federal government. On this program, ABC News will piece together what we know and where the breakdowns occurred.

Born as a garden-variety tropical depression, Katrina grew into a tropical storm and officially earned hurricane status on August 24, 2005. It initially made landfall north of Miami, causing serious flooding and eleven deaths. But only when it marched across the Florida peninsula and hit the warm waters of the Gulf of Mexico did Katrina rapidly intensify and unleash its full fury. And as it evolved into a monster storm, the National Hurricane Center issued pointed warnings to the target communities along the Gulf Coast. The director made phone calls to key officials, including the mayor of New Orleans, saying Katrina could be "the big one" officials had long feared. Simultaneously, weather service bulletins were issued with unusually apocalyptic language. One predicted a storm of "unprecedented strength," "the area will be uninhabitable for weeks," and went on to predict human suffering "incredible by modern standards."

Given the dire warnings, should the deaths and suffering throughout the Gulf region have been as great? Were the recommendations issued by the 9/11 Commission put into practice? Ted Koppel hosts a *Primetime* special edition, "Moment of Crisis: System Failure," a moment by-moment chronology of what went so terribly wrong in the horrific days following Katrina's strike on the Gulf Coast. This was America's first major test of emergency response since 9/11, a test that has received failing grades.

### *Critical Thinking Questions*

1. In "Moment of Crisis—System Failure," state and local officials blame federal officials for the grossly inadequate response to this natural disaster and federal officials blame state and local officials. What are the responsibilities of the federal government, particularly agencies such as FEMA and the Department of Homeland

Security, in regard to both natural and man-made disasters? What are the responsibilities of state and local governments?

2. How much of a role did poverty play in the tragic aftermath of Hurricane Katrina? Do you get the impression from viewing the program that race had any impact on the way the federal government responded to the crisis?

3. Could this disaster have been averted simply by reinforcing New Orleans' levee system years ago as a preventive measure? Does the federal government have an obligation to maintain and update the infrastructure in places such as New Orleans or is this the responsibility of state and local governments?

4. Does the Constitution provide any guidance on whether the response to disasters such as Hurricane Katrina should be orchestrated at the federal level or at the state and local levels?

5. In light of the response to Hurricane Katrina, what can be said about American federalism both in theory and in practice? Would a stronger federal government have been better equipped to deal with the crisis, or was the inadequate response an isolated case of mismanagement that does not reflect upon the basic structure of the U.S. government?

## REPORT CARD
**Originally Aired: 10/8/03**
**Program: *Nightline***
**Running Time: 17:24**

Public education is one of the great promises of this country. But is America keeping that promise? This *ABC News* program offers a timely report card on the nation's public education system. Hard hit by state budget cuts in recent years, the system is also under immense pressure from the No Child Left Behind initiative—legislation that demands much of schools but, say critics, provides little funding to help them meet the mandated goals. Visits to a school in Arlington, Massachusetts, and The University of Texas at Austin amply illustrate the hard realities of faculties being slashed and class sizes swelling…and the promise of public education steadily fading.

### *Critical Thinking Questions*
1. What is an unfunded mandate? Give examples of unfunded mandates in the No Child Left Behind Act that are discussed in "Report Card."

2. In "Report Card," author Jonathan Kozol says the "way we finance education in the United States is archaic, chaotic, and utterly undemocratic." What about our education financing leads him to say this?

3. States have raised a number of objections to federal education standards. Briefly discuss two objections that states might have.

# CHAPTER 4
## PUBLIC OPINION AND THE MASS MEDIA

## CHAPTER OVERVIEW

Chapter 4 examines how U.S. citizens form opinions on political issues and identifies political culture and political socialization as important elements in the study of public opinion.

The chapter defines public opinion as the range of opinions expressed by members of a community on any subject, and political opinion as the range of opinions expressed on political issues.

The chapter introduces techniques of polling, survey research, and focus groups, which are used by politicians, public officials, polling organizations, and scholars to identify what the public is thinking and to predict the outcome of elections. Criticisms of public opinion polling and survey research are also presented.

The chapter reviews the nature and role of the media in U.S. politics, including media coverage of elections, television advertising, the question of media bias, and the introduction of new media sources such as cable television, the Internet and Web logs. Proposals for reforming the role of the media in elections are also discussed.

The chapter concludes with an examination of how public opinion translates into political action and identifies citizens of higher social and economic status as more likely to participate in political activities than citizens of lower social and economic status.

## LEARNING OBJECTIVES

1. Define political socialization, outline the main factors that affect political socialization, and assess their relative influence in the socialization process.
2. Define political culture and explain the relationship between political culture and political socialization.
3. Outline the factors that must be considered when conducting a scientific poll.
4. Compare and contrast the different types of polls, including the purpose and process of administering each.
5. Assess the criticisms of public opinion polling and outline the mechanisms by which such criticisms can be overcome.
6. Discuss candidates' use of the new media and assess the effects of the news media on recent national campaigns.
7. Explain the main forms of political participation.

## CHAPTER OUTLINE

I. The American political culture
   A. Fundamental commitment to democratic values
   B. Importance of commitment to democratic goals and procedures among political leaders
II. Political socialization
   A. Process of transmission of political culture from one generation to the next

B. Agents of political socialization
   1. The family
   2. The school
   3. The peer group
   4. The media
   5. Social class: income, occupation, and education
   6. Race and religion
   7. Place of residence
   8. History and political events

III.   The nature of public opinion
A. General features
   1. Intensity
   2. Concentration
   3. Stability
   4. Distribution
   5. Salience

IV.   Measuring public opinion
A. Scientific polling
B. How polls are conducted
   1. Sampling and survey research
   2. Telephone polls
   3. Exit polls
   4. Focus groups
C. Criticisms of public opinion polling
   1. Problems related to the sample
   2. Problems associated with the phrasing of questions (see Ashcroft example)
   3. Special problems with primary election and exit polls
   4. The growth of the media

V.   The media: Newspapers, radio, and television
A. Roles of the media
   1. The media as reporter
   2. The media as agenda-setter
   3. The media as investigator
B. The media and elections
C. Television advertising
D. The question of media bias
   1. Editor versus reporters
   2. Media ownership
E. The new media: Cable television
F. F.   The Internet
   1. Campaigning
   2. Fundraising
G. Proposals for reform

VI.   How Americans participate
A. Forms and rates of participation
B. Characteristics of political participants
C. Consequences of political participation

# CHAPTER SUMMARY

Public opinion must be viewed within the context of the nation's political culture. Political culture in the United States is based on fundamental, widely supported values of democracy, including equality, individual freedom, and due process of law. The democratic beliefs of citizens are passed on from generation to generation through political socialization. The important influences in political socialization include family, school, peer groups, media, social class, race, religion, geography, history, and personal experiences.

Political opinion is the set of opinions expressed by the community on the political issues of the day. Some general features of political opinions are intensity, concentration, stability, distribution, and salience. Some political opinions are short-lived, whereas others are more enduring. Core attitudes, such as whether a person is liberal or conservative, may remain basically the same throughout his/her life.

Measuring public opinion helps politicians and public officials know what the public is thinking about issues and candidates. Techniques for measuring public opinion have become more scientific since polling began in 1944. The basic elements of modern scientific polling are the survey and the sample.

Critics charge that scientific polling is flawed because of problems related to sampling and because of problems with the way questions are sometimes phrased. Primary election and exit polling are viewed as especially problematic. Despite the alleged problems with polling, polls have become a central element of politics in the United States.

The media have always played an important part in U.S. politics, and the media's potential to influence public opinion and political leaders is significant. The media fulfill a variety of functions, including socialization and entertainment, and they directly interact with the political sphere in the roles of reporting, agenda-setting, and investigating.

In covering elections, the media tend to focus on the horse race rather than the policies and issues being discussed in the campaign. There are differences across types of media, however. For example, the electronic media present much less news than the print media, and radio news programs give greater coverage to political events.

National political campaigns rely heavily on television advertising. TV advertising typically accounts for two-thirds of the budget in a statewide campaign, although the importance and cost of television advertising varies across campaigns and regions of the country. Recent political campaigns have witnessed an increase in negative advertising, which is based on ads that attack a candidate's opponent.

Since the 1990s, presidential campaigns have increasingly turned to cable television outlets, as the national networks have experienced declining ratings and viewers have moved to cable television. Many candidates have turned to nontraditional media such as cable news shows, which have provided attractive alternatives to candidates who dislike their treatment by traditional media or want to have alternative media outlets. The Internet and e-mail have also become sources of communication and information in political campaigns and politics. Major political parties and many political candidates use websites to fund-raise, recruit, and advertise their opinion on public issues. Additionally, Web logs, or blogs, have become a popular source of information for voters to share and discuss their political views.

The increasing dependence of political campaigns on the media worries many critics who warn that style is becoming more important than substance. Attempts and proposed attempts to reform the process through legislation have failed to address concerns about the superficiality of political campaigns. Rather, fundamental changes in U.S. culture and civic education may be required to improve America's political discourse.

For public opinion to influence our system of government, people must act on their political views by voting, working for candidates, contributing money to campaigns, or attending political meetings. Those with higher social and economic status, however, tend to participate more than those of lower social and economic status. Political participation is likely to result in more favorable action by government officials, and those who participate often obtain the most benefits from the government.

## KEY TERMS

blogs
exit poll
muckrakers
political culture
political opinion
political socialization
public opinion

sampling
scientific polling
survey research
telephone polls
tracking poll
yellow journalism

## PRACTICE EXERCISES

### FILL IN THE BLANKS

1.    The basic, widely supported values that hold society together and legitimize a nation's political institutions are known as _____ _____.

2.    The transmission of political values from one generation to another is referred to as _____ _____.

3.    Almost as great as the influence of one's family, the _____ is also believed to have a great impact on the socialization process.

4.    The process of choosing a relatively small number of cases to be studied for information about the larger population from which they have been selected is called _____.

5.    A polling method that shows day-to-day changes in voter preferences preceding an election is called a(n) _____ poll.

6.    A polling method in which voters are interviewed at the polls on Election Day is called a(n) _____ poll.

7.    Newspaper coverage that focuses on sensational stories and scandals is commonly referred to as _____ _____.

8.    Late-nineteenth-century journalists who exposed corruption in government and industry were called _____.

9.    Because people tend to remember short, punchy messages, the _____ _____ has become a key feature of television coverage of political campaigns.

10.    The media are often accused by both Republicans and Democrats of offering _____ coverage of the news.

MULTIPLE CHOICE

11. The earliest and perhaps most important influence in political socialization is
    a. place of residence.
    b. family.
    c. peer group.
    d. television and other media.

12. On which of the following issues is public opinion likely to be more concentrated?
    a. crime
    b. education
    c. taxation
    d. farm subsidies

13. People _____ tend to be more conservative in their political opinions.
    a. with higher incomes
    b. with lower incomes
    c. in unskilled jobs
    d. with little education

14. The political party that dominated the South for the century following the Civil War was the
    a. Republican party.
    b. Libertarian party.
    c. Democratic party.
    d. Constitution party.

15. Salience is a feature of political opinions that refers to
    a. how often an opinion changes.
    b. the types of people who support various positions on an issue.
    c. the portion of the population that holds a certain viewpoint.
    d. the importance of an issue to a person or group.

16. Julio has been selected by the Gallup organization as one of 1,500 voters who are interviewed by telephone and asked to express their vote choice in the upcoming presidential election. Julio is part of
    a. a peer research group.
    b. a survey sample.
    c. a focus group.
    d. an exit poll.

17. A(n) _____ poll is conducted every day during the week leading up to an election in order to determine day-to-day changes in voter preferences.
    a. exit
    b. focus
    c. tracking
    d. temperature

18. A technique that has become widely used in campaigns, in which a group of about 12 people are asked their views about political candidates and issues, is called
a. a tracking group.
b. an exit group.
c. a focus group.
d. a survey group.

19. Accurate polls in primary elections are
a. especially difficult because turnout in primary elections is typically very low.
b. especially difficult because turnout in primary elections is typically close to 100 percent.
c. easier to obtain than accurate polls in general elections.
d. easier to obtain because of the extensive media coverage of primary campaigns.

20. When the media brings issues to the attention of the public through news coverage, they are fulfilling their role as
a. yellow journalists.
b. muckrakers.
c. agenda-setters.
d. reporters.

21. In covering elections, the media tend to focus on
a. the candidates' standings in the polls.
b. candidates who have never held elected office.
c. lesser known candidates.
d. the issues being discussed in the campaign.

22. A controversial aspect of media bias that has arisen in recent years is
a. the increase in liberal journalists and editors.
b. the increase in conservative journalists and editors.
c. increasing concentration of news outlets in the hands of a few corporate entities.
d. the increase in smaller local and national cable stations that provide information to the public.

23. The use of the Internet in the 1996 presidential election campaign centered on providing candidate information to potential voters; today, however, its most important use is for campaign
a. fund-raising.
b. advertising.
c. volunteer recruitment.
d. paraphernalia sales.

24. Of the following, who is most likely to participate in politics?
a. someone with a high school education, but no college
b. someone with a college education
c. someone who is unemployed
d. someone who is a member of a racial minority group

25. For participation activities such as working for a political party, attending a public meeting, and belonging to a political club, participation rates are generally
a. above 75 percent
b. between 50-74 percent
c. between 25-49 percent
d. less than 10 percent

## TRUE OR FALSE

26. Political leaders in the United States are more likely than the general public to support democratic goals and procedures.
T  F

27. Race and religion typically have very little influence on a person's political opinions.
T  F

28. Focus groups are more useful than survey research for providing information about a representative sample of voters.
T  F

29. In the 2004 presidential election, bloggers released the inaccurate results of exit polls on the Internet.
T  F

30. Government officials typically implement public policies that benefit voters and non-voters equally.
T  F

## DISCUSSION, ESSAY

31. Identify and discuss examples of how political culture and political socialization influence political opinion.

32. Discuss the process of political socialization and identify important influences in your own political socialization.

33. Discuss the importance of measuring public opinion in a representative democracy.

34. Provide examples of problems associated with public opinion polls.

35. Discuss how the growing reliance on new media and the Internet to obtain information is important in politics today.

36. Identify and evaluate proposals for reforming political campaigns. Which reforms, if any, would be most beneficial? Why?

37.     How has September 11 and its aftermath affected American thinking about issues of war and foreign policy?

38.     What role did the Internet blogs play during the 2004 presidential election?


## ABC NEWS/PRENTICE HALL VIDEO LIBRARY: AMERICAN GOVERNMENT

**MASS MEDIA**
**Q & A**
**Originally Aired: 4/28/05**
**Program: *Nightline***

Every year, at more or less the same time, the president gets to address the nation—and the world—on his vision for the coming term. Where we are and where we're going. What he intends to do. How does he take all the issues—from social security to gay marriage, from Iraq to Iran, from the nuclear threat to terrorism—and figure out what gets priority? On this program, we talk to some people who have worked closely with presidents and who have actually written many of the State of the Union speeches. We'll see what goes into the address and what the president is actually trying to say. One of our panelists is a consultant on the popular TV show *West Wing*. Over the years, they've tried to give the audience a behind-the scenes look at the frenzied jockeying and preparation that goes into this yearly address. We hope our panel will tell us whether the television show comes close.

A veteran of hard-nosed politics, Mary Matalin has most recently served as an assistant to President Bush and as counselor to Vice President Cheney. Michael Waldman was President Bill Clinton's chief speechwriter from 1995 to 1999. He cranked out 2,000 speeches for the president, including many of the State of the Union addresses. Ken Duberstein was President Ronald Reagan's chief of staff from 1988-1989. He's also a consultant to *West Wing*. Ted Koppel joins this panel prior to the 2005 State of the Union address to try to pick apart what the president does. They'll view a few scenes from previous *West Wing* episodes to see how close their storylines come to reality. Who does he hear from? What are the issues that get into the speech? How important is every adjective and every adverb? There are fights, literally, over every single word and issue that go into the speech. It's a statement of intent for the year. And this one is particularly important during a volatile period in this country's history. It will be interesting to see what President Bush sets out to do on the heels of his victory in November. After we record the first part of the conversation, we'll review the speech, and then come back to our panelists to see how President Bush did. What were the surprises? How was the tone? What did he focus on? Was it a wide-ranging and all-encompassing speech or a narrowly focused one?

### *Critical Thinking Questions*

1. Briefly compare press conferences with the U.S. president and press conferences with the British prime minister.

2. Why do the reporters in "Q & A" believe U.S. presidents are not questioned as aggressively as are the leaders of other countries?

3. While the number of presidential addresses and appearances has grown dramatically in the last 50 years, the number of presidential press conferences has dropped just as dramatically. Why might this be so?

## AMERICA IN BLACK & WHITE
**Originally Aired: 9/24/96**
**Program: *Nightline***
**Running Time: 14:54**

Discusses black and white issues concerning local television news reporting.

### *Critical Thinking Questions*
1. After studying local TV stations in Philadelphia, what conclusions did an Annenberg study draw about coverage based on race?

2. What guidelines did an Austin TV station put into place to avoid negative racial stereotypes in its reporting?

3. While most experts agree the media have the power to shape public opinion, there are some factors that limit media influence. Briefly discuss a few of these factors that might apply to local TV coverage of race.

# CHAPTER 5
## POLITICAL PARTIES AND INTEREST GROUPS

## CHAPTER OVERVIEW

Chapter 5 focuses on organized political activity and how groups participate in politics in the United States. The chapter begins by distinguishing between political parties and interest groups. The chapter then details the functions and goals of political parties and describes the two-party system and party competition in the United States. Minor parties, the structure of political parties, party identification among voters, and the role of the party in the legislative branch of government are also discussed.

Chapter 5 then focuses on interest groups. After providing a definition of interest groups, the growth and structure of interest groups in the United States is discussed and different types of interest groups are identified. The chapter identifies the activities of interest groups and briefly examines the funding sources of such groups. The chapter concludes with a brief discussion of the power of interest groups and the regulations designed to limit their power.

## LEARNING OBJECTIVES

1. Define the main features and purpose of political parties.
2. Define the main features and purpose of interest groups.
3. Compare and contrast interest groups and political parties.
4. Describe the features that define the U.S. two-party system.
5. Outline the reasons why the United States has a two-party system, contrasting the U.S. model with other democratic political systems.
6. Assess the methods interest groups use to exert influence on the decision making process.
7. Formulate reasons for the decline in voter identification with political parties and the consequences for the American political process.

## CHAPTER OUTLINE

I.      Political parties
        A. Historical relationship to democracy in the United States
        B. Functions
            1. Recruit and select leaders
            2. Represent interest groups
            3. Educate the public on issues
            4. Serve as a check on the majority party
            5. Provide a degree of order and predictability in the political process
II.     The American two-party system
        A. Traits
            1. Two-party system
            2. Long periods of single-party dominance
        B. Explanations for the U.S. two-party system
            1. Institutional theory
            2. Historical explanation

        3. Cultural explanation

     C. Party competition

        1. Variability

        2. One-party dominance in particular locations

        3. Divided government

     D. The nature of American political parties

        1. Two-party system

        2. Decentralization of power

        3. Coalitions of groups

        4. Ideological diversity

     E. Minor parties (example—Nader and Green Party in 2000)

        1. Organization

           a. Political ideology

           b. Issues

        2. Origins

III.    The structure of political parties

     A. The national parties

        1. The national convention

        2. The national committee

        3. The national chair

     B. The state and local parties

        1. The county committee

        2. City, township, and precinct committees

     C. Decentralization of party power

IV.    Parties and voters: The decline of party identification

     A. Possible reasons for the decline in party identification

        1. Realignment theory

        2. Dealignment theory

        3. More evidence supports dealignment than realignment theory

     B. Effects of the decline of party identification

V.    The party in the legislature

     A. The party's lack of control in Congress

     B. Influence of the party on voting in Congress

VI.    Reform or status quo?

     A. Criticisms of the American two-party system

     B. Proposals for reform of the political party system

VII.    Interest groups

     A. The growth of interest groups

        1. Reasons for the increase in the number of interest groups

           a. Federalism and separation of powers encourages group activity

           b. Economic specialization of American society

           c. Success of older interest groups

     B. The structure of interest groups

     C. Types of interest groups

        1. Economic interest groups (business, unions, etc.)

        2. Noneconomic interest groups (NOW as one example)

        3. Single-issue groups (Sierra Club)

        4. Political action committees (PACs)

D. Activities of interest groups
1. Lobbying Congress
2. Lobbying the executive branch
3. Interest groups and the courts
4. Grassroots activities
5. Electoral support
E. Funding of interest groups
1. Corporate budgets for lobbying activities
2. Dues, gifts, donations, grants
3. Staff-generated revenues
4. Financial investments and endowments
F. How powerful are interest groups?
1. Uneven distribution of power
2. Criticisms of interest groups
3. Efforts to limit the power of interest groups
4. Changing the rules that govern lobbyists

## CHAPTER SUMMARY

Organized political activity in the United States is based on the activity of groups. Two basic types of groups that participate in politics are political parties and interest groups. Political parties participate by getting their members elected to office. They have existed throughout the nation's history. They perform multiple functions, including informing the public, selecting political candidates, and serving as a check on the opposing party.

The two-party system has been with us since George Washington's second term. The institutional theory holds that America has been a two-party country because the winner-take-all process punishes minority parties. The historical explanation for the U.S. two-party system is based on the tendency of institutions to preserve their initial form. The first political issue to divide the nation was the ratification of the Constitution, which divided the nation into two groups. The historical explanation sees this pattern of division into two groups as persisting over time. The cultural explanation for the two-party system focuses on the ability of distinct racial, religious, and ethnic groups to join one of the two major parties in coalition with other groups, rather than to form different parties to represent distinct group interests.

Despite the nation's two-party system, some geographical areas have been dominated by a single party. This may be due to a local basis for party loyalty, or because the majority of the people of a given area are very similar, thus, they do not need multiple parties to represent their interests.

Political parties in the United States are highly decentralized. The national parties are weak, and state and local political parties are much stronger. Political parties in the United States are based on coalitions of distinct groups, and they are ideologically diverse. This diversity tends to produce moderation.

Over long periods of history, many citizens have identified strongly with one of the two major parties. Following the Civil War, there was intense loyalty to the Republican party. Following the New Deal, the Democratic party enjoyed majority support from the electorate. In the past 50 years, there has been a decline in identification with the political parties and an increase in the number of independent voters. The political parties in Congress are also relatively weak, and for those who see parties as essential to the preservation of democratic government, the weakness of the political parties in the United States is a source of concern.

A second source of group activity in the United States is the interest group. Interest groups have existed throughout the history of the United States, but there has been an explosion in the number of interest groups since the 1970s. Interest groups try to influence the political system by shaping public opinion, opposing and supporting political candidates, and lobbying government officials.

There are a number of different types of interest groups, including economic interest groups, noneconomic interest groups, single-issue groups, and political action committees, or PACs. The main way that interest groups affect public policy is through lobbying: working to convince legislators to vote a certain way on proposed legislation. Lobbyists also seek to influence policy in the executive branch. Interest groups also use lawsuits, electoral support, and grassroots activities to influence public opinion.

The power of interest groups is not evenly divided, and the power and influence of some groups has led to attempts to limit the influence of interest groups. Supporters of interest group activity argue that interest groups have increased participation in the political process. Unlike political parties, interest groups are not responsible for the success or failure of government programs enacted by party members in government, and supporters of stronger parties argue that interest group activity decreases accountability and responsibility among elected officials.

## KEY TERMS

| | |
|---|---|
| *amicus curiae* brief | political action committee (PAC) |
| Independents | political parties |
| interest group | precinct |
| lobbying | professional association |
| minor parties | single-issue interest group |
| multiparty systems | trade association |
| national chair | two-party system |
| national committee | ward |
| national convention | |
| party identification | |
| party unity votes | |

## PRACTICE EXERCISES

### FILL IN THE BLANKS

1.  In the 2006 election, the _____ party, with aid of two Independent members, gained control of both houses of Congress, reestablishing divided government.

2.  By the time John Adams was elected as president in 1796, America had already become a _____ system.

3.  The explanation for the U.S. two-party system that emphasizes the influence of the single-member district method of choosing legislators is called the _____ theory.

4.  The first two major parties in U.S. politics were the Democratic-Republicans and the _____.

5. The _____ party was represented by Ralph Nader in 2000.

6. Individuals who do not identify with a political party are called _____.

7. A situation in which voters change their party loyalties to new party allegiances, as occurred after the election of 1932, is known as _____.

8. A period during which party identification weakens causing political parties to decline is known as _____.

9. In the past, most interest groups formed around _____ interests.

10. _____ and trade associations have created the largest portion of today's political action committees.

## MULTIPLE CHOICE

11. The historical explanation for the U.S. two-party system is based on
    a. the tendency of institutions to preserve their initial form.
    b. the development of weak third parties throughout U.S. history.
    c. group diversity in the United States.
    d. the single-member district method for congressional elections.

12. An important factor contributing to the decline of state party organizations was the
    a. national nominating convention.
    b. national party platform.
    c. civil service system.
    d. popular election of senators.

13. Many democratic nations have a _____ system, in which a number of parties compete successfully for public office.
    a. unitary
    b. candidate-centered
    c. multiparty
    d. two-party

14. Loyalty of voters toward a political party is called party
    a. realignment.
    b. identification.
    c. deregulation.
    d. competition.

15. Compared to a parliamentary system, political parties in the United States tend to be
    a. much less influential in nominating candidates to represent their party.
    b. much more influential in nominating candidates to represent their party.
    c. more likely to control both the executive and legislative branches.
    d. more likely to control both the legislative and judicial branches.

16. In America, minor parties exist primarily to
a. advance their own ideas by opposing the programs and policies of the two main parties.
b. hold national leaders accountable.
c. submit campaign contributions on the behalf of the two main parties.
d. "train" candidates before they attempt to participate in one of the larger party elections.

17. Interest groups are similar to political parties in that both
a. elect leadership from among members of Congress to represent their interests in Congress.
b. provide a label to identify candidates for public office on ballots.
c. are formally organized, with a definite structure and set of regulations.
d. use their strength to win benefits from government.

18. The classic political party "machine" provided immigrants with many essential services, and in return they demanded
a. money and labor.
b. money and loyalty.
c. loyalty and labor.
d. loyalty and votes.

19. A(n) _____ is the process by which the voting public directly chooses a party's candidate for the general election.
a. indirect primary
b. direct primary
c. open primary
d. closed primary

20. Several proposals for reform of America's political party system have been made. Of the following, which is *not* considered a reason for reform?
a. The major two-party candidates are too similar and so offer no real choice to the electorate.
b. The party system has too much control over candidates after they are elected.
c. The party system has no control over candidates once they are elected.
d. The major two-party candidates are too extreme, representing few of the electorate and offering no representation to the majority.

21. Interest group activity has grown over time due to all of the following reasons except:
a. new groups have formed as a result of America's economic specialization.
b. new groups have formed as a result of other groups' successful lobbying.
c. new groups have formed to represent majority interests in society.
d. new groups have formed to increase lobbying activity at multiple levels of government.

22. U.S. trade union membership has decreased over time, mostly due to
a. a lack of government support.
b. the declining importance of manufacturing in the U.S.
c. employees' lack of trust in trade union leadership.
d. the increased representation of laborers in Congress.

23. An example of the grassroots activities of interests groups is
   a. a PAC contribution to a congressional campaign.
   b. an interest group advertisement aimed at influencing public views on a particular issue.
   c. filing an *amicus curiae* brief.
   d. testifying before a congressional committee on an issue of concern to the group.

24. The primary reason for limiting the amount of money that PACs can contribute to campaigns is
   a. to limit the amount of influence the PAC can have on elected officials.
   b. to control the overall costs of campaigns.
   c. to ensure that large sums of money aren't wasted.
   d. to force candidates to support their campaigns with their own money.

25. A criticism of interest groups relative to political parties is that
   a. interest groups are quicker to compromise than political parties.
   b. interest groups promote greater accountability than parties.
   c. political parties better enable individuals to choose the problem that most concerns them.
   d. unlike political parties, interest groups are not responsible for the success or failure of government programs.


TRUE OR FALSE

26. One must be a member of an interest group to benefit from its activities.
   T  F

27. Interest groups often lobby the courts for favorable decisions in cases that concern them.
   T  F

28. Grassroots lobbying is best directed at legislators who are undecided about a particular issue.
   T  F

29. When interest groups hold demonstrations they do so to gain the attention of the media and to raise public awareness and support for their views.
   T  F

30. The number of interest groups in the United States has declined in recent decades.
   T  F


DISCUSSION, ESSAY

31. Identify and describe the major functions of political parties in the United States.

32. Outline the structure of political parties at the national, state, and local levels.

33. Describe the role of political parties in the operation of the legislature, and identify the differences between legislative parties in the United States and parties in parliamentary systems.

34. Distinguish among different types of interest groups, and discuss the relative power of distinct types of groups.

35. Identify and evaluate criticisms of interest group influence in U.S. politics.


## ABC NEWS/PRENTICE HALL VIDEO LIBRARY: AMERICAN GOVERNMENT

**GOD AND COUNTRY**
**Originally Aired: 11/26/02**
**Program: *Nightline***
**Running Time: 12:41**

Over the last couple of years, what has come to be called the Christian Right has become more and more active in supporting the Sharon government in its war with the Palestinians. And their political clout with the Bush administration is considerable. They are opposed to giving the Palestinians any land, taking a much harder line than many Americans. The reason? Prophecy. Many believe that what is playing out now in the Middle East is all part of the process leading toward the Second Coming. The existence of the state of Israel is crucial to that process and many believe that Israel must cover all of the land, including the occupied territories, in order for this process to move forward. So they send money, take trips to Israel, meet regularly with Israeli officials, including Sharon, and at the same time seem to be breaking what was a strong alliance between American Jews and the Democratic party. That would certainly change the political landscape in this country as well. Israel needs friends now, [as it is] facing serious criticism from much of the world over its tactics in the current conflict. And so both sides are sort of glossing over a theological issue. According to the prophecies that many Christians believe, as part of the Second Coming, Jews will have the opportunity to either convert to Christianity, or perish. In other words, they will disappear as a people, or religion, one way or the other. You might think that this would be a point of contention between the two religions but it doesn't appear to be. Ted Koppel interviews Pat Robertson, founder and chairman of the Christian Broadcasting Network. He is a former presidential candidate and arguably one of the most recognized leaders of the evangelical Christian community.

### *Critical Thinking Questions*
1. In "God and Country," conservative Christians explain their strong support for Israel, especially their support of Jewish occupation of the West Bank. Briefly discuss the reasons they give for this support.

2. Not all Jews welcome the support of conservative American Christians. What implications of that support concern them?

3. As a general rule, interest groups rarely have a decisive role in the formulation of foreign policy. How might conservative Christian support for Israel be an exception to that rule?

CHAPTER 6
NOMINATIONS AND ELECTIONS


CHAPTER OVERVIEW

Chapter 6 focuses on the processes of nominations, campaigns, elections, and voting in the United States. The chapter begins by presenting a history of the various methods that have been used in the process of nominations. In the early years of the nation, candidates for elective office were chosen by a process called the legislative caucus. The legislative caucus was followed by the development of the mixed caucus, the convention, and the primary system. The nomination process for presidential candidates is distinct from the process for other elected offices, and the chapter reviews the details of this process. It also stresses the importance of frontloading in the primary/caucus process, a process that will continue into 2008, making it difficult for relatively unknown candidates to emerge as choices for primary voters.

The chapter identifies the importance of campaign finance in the U.S. electoral process and reviews the development of current laws regarding campaign finance. In 2002, a new campaign finance reform law was passed banning soft money contributions to national political parties, limiting issue-related ads on TV while raising hard money contributions. This 2002 legislation led to the emergence of 527 committees which are exempt from the soft money ban, causing them to become major players in the 2004 election period. The chapter also discusses campaign strategy and televised debates.

The chapter next describes the procedures for voter registration, balloting, and the Electoral College (the 2004 presidential election is noted) and identifies important elements of congressional elections, including the results of the 2006 election which produced a gain in six seats for the Democrats in the Senate and 31 in the House of Representatives. The chapter explains the advantages of incumbency and how the lack of competitive congressional races has prompted a call for term limits.

The chapter concludes with a consideration of voter turnout and voter choice and the factors associated with turnout and choice of candidate. It also mentions legislation introduced in 2002 and passed in 2004 meant to control campaign finance in the United States.


LEARNING OBJECTIVES

1. Describe the process whereby the president is elected.
2. Outline the criticisms of the Electoral College.
3. Compare and contrast the presidential primary and the caucus systems. Assess the advantages and disadvantages of each system.
4. Explain the congressional election process.
5. Summarize campaign finance legislation and assess the reasons for the limited success in reforming campaign finance.
6. Compare and contrast office-block and party-column balloting.
7. Explain the reasons why Americans do not vote and assess the implications of nonvoting for the American political system.
8. Outline the demographic and ideological characteristics that influence how Americans vote.

# CHAPTER OUTLINE

I.  Nomination procedures
    A. Historical overview
        1. Legislative caucus
        2. Mixed caucus
        3. Convention system
    B. Present system
        1. Types of primaries
            a. Closed
            b. Open

II.  Nominating a presidential candidate
    A. Choosing the delegates
        1. Presidential primaries
        2. Caucuses and conventions
    B. The preconvention campaign
        1. Winning early state primaries
        2. New Hampshire primary and Iowa caucus
        3. Frontloading in 2004 and 2008
    C. The national convention
        1. Adopting a platform
        2. Nominating a presidential candidate
        3. Nominating a vice presidential candidate
        4. A national primary?

III.  The campaign
    A. Campaign financing
    B. Campaign finance legislation
        1. The Federal Election Campaign Act of 1974
            a. Soft money
            b. Hard money
        2. Campaign Finance Reform Act of 2002
            a. The emergence of 527 committees and their effect on the 2004 election
        3. Congressional campaigns
    C. Campaign strategy
    D. Television debates

IV.  The election
    A. Registration
    B. Balloting
        1. Office-block ballot
        2. Party-column ballot
        3. Absentee ballot
    C. Selecting the president and vice president: The Electoral College
        1. Problems with the Electoral College
        2. Reform or abolition?
    D. Congressional elections

V.  How Americans vote (and don't vote)
    A. Who votes?
    B. How do Americans vote?

# CHAPTER SUMMARY

In most democratic nations, political parties choose the candidates for public office. The United States, however, uses a process that is designed to give voters greater power to choose the candidates. The most common method of nominating candidates is the direct primary, in which candidates are selected by the voters in a primary election. States that do not use primaries use a caucus or convention system, where party members meet to choose the candidates for the party.

The process for nominating presidential candidates is different from that used to nominate candidates for other offices. Formally, the nominations for the presidential candidates of the Republican and Democratic parties occur at the national conventions of the two parties. The conventions, however, reflect the results of primary elections (and, to a far lesser extent, caucuses) held in each state. The primary process differs from state to state and between the two parties. The process is the same, however, in that the results of the primaries determine the delegates who will attend the Republican and Democratic nominating conventions in the summer before the election, and the primaries determine which candidates these delegates will support for the nomination.

In recent elections, states have moved the dates of their primaries to earlier in the election year, because early primaries influence later primaries and the nominees may already be identified before the primaries of states with later dates. The effect of this has been to reduce the duration of the nomination process. In 2000, both the Republican and Democratic party nominees were known by March 15. Frontloading in 2004 also made it more difficult for unknown candidates to gain their party's nomination and, since then, several additional states have adopted earlier primary dates.

In addition to formally nominating the presidential candidate of the party, the party convention also nominates the vice presidential candidate. Typically, the presidential candidate chooses a vice presidential running mate, and the convention approves this choice. The other major task of the party conventions is to adopt a party platform. The party platform is a statement of the policy positions of the party in a range of policy areas. Statements about different issue areas are called planks.

After the national conventions, presidential campaigns begin. The political parties raise campaign finances from a relatively small number of wealthy contributors. Since the 1950s, the increasing use of television has greatly raised the cost of campaigns. After serious violations of campaign finance laws in the 1972 presidential election, new legislation was passed to establish public financing of presidential campaigns and contribution limits on various sources. In 2002, a new campaign finance reform law banned soft money contributions to the national political parties, a law that had an unforeseen consequence which emerged during the 2004 election as groups exempt from the soft money ban (527 organizations) emerged to support candidates with more than $550 million.

There is no public funding of congressional campaigns, and incumbents benefit from the current system of campaign finance. House members, who must run every two years, are especially concerned with fundraising.

In campaigning for office, the candidates of the two major parties usually adopt different strategies. Democratic candidates usually stress party unity and getting out the vote, while Republican candidates stress their individual merits. A candidate who is seeking to defeat an incumbent will inevitably attack the incumbent's record. Based on the Electoral College system, presidential elections are won or lost in the most populous states, and presidential candidates are particularly focused on winning these states to ensure a victory in the Electoral College.

The Electoral College system is outlined in the Constitution. The members of the Electoral College are elected every four years under procedures established by state law. In the early years of the nation, the electors were chosen by state legislatures, but this system has been replaced by one that ties the Electoral College vote of a state to the popular vote in the state. The Electoral College system has been criticized as anti-democratic, but proposals for changing the system have not gained adequate support for changes to occur. Even the disputed presidential election of 2000 between Bush and Gore, where the latter won the popular vote but lost the Electoral College, did not spark national momentum to change the system.

Incumbent members of Congress have a distinct advantage in running for reelection, and the competitiveness of House races in particular has declined over time as would-be challengers recognize the low likelihood of beating an incumbent. One result of this has been a call for term limits. The Supreme Court, however, has found term limits for Congress to be unconstitutional.

The most common form of political activity for U.S. citizens is voting. Yet only about 50 percent of the electorate has chosen to vote in recent presidential elections, and even fewer vote in congressional elections. The 1996 presidential election turnout was the lowest since 1924. In 2000, only 51 percent of eligible voters voted for president. While voter turnout increased to 59 percent in the 2004 election, voter turnout is still lower than its all-time high, 70 percent, in the mid 1800s. Young people, minority group members, and people with less education are among those who are least likely to vote.

Social scientists have long been interested in how citizens choose which political party and candidates to support. Voters with higher levels of income and education, white Protestants, and men tend to support Republican candidates. Voters with lower levels of income and education, women, blacks, Hispanics, Catholic, and Jewish voters are more likely to support Democratic candidates. Close to one-third of the electorate identify themselves as independent and not affiliated with either the Democratic or Republican parties.

## KEY TERMS

| | |
|---|---|
| ballot | national convention |
| caucuses | open primary |
| closed primary | party platform |
| coattail effect | presidential primary |
| convention | primary |
| Electoral College | primary registration |
| frontloading | runoff primary |
| hard money | soft money |
| | voter turnout |

## PRACTICE EXERCISES

## FILL IN THE BLANKS

1.  Today, the _____ system is the most common method of nominating individuals for public office in the United States.

2.  Andrew Jackson and his supporters favored the _____ system for presidential nominations.

3.    A primary election, in which only voters who have registered with a particular party may vote in that party's primary, is called a(n) _____ primary.

4.    The _____ effect refers to the rallying of delegates around the primary candidate who experiences a number of primary victories and high opinion poll ratings.

5.    Of the two major parties in U.S. elections, the _____ party is usually able to outspend the other, largely because more wealthy people support them.

6.    The 2002 campaign finance reform law banned _____ money contributions to the national political parties.

7.    The _____ _____ _____ Act (1993) was enacted to simplify voter registration and increase voter turnout.

8.    If no presidential candidate receives a majority of votes in the Electoral College, the president is chosen from among the candidates with the three highest electoral vote totals by the _____.

9.    A _____ district can be defined as an area in which one party always wins at least 55 percent of the vote and the other party never obtains more than 45 percent.

10.   Historically, and with few exceptions, the president's party will lose congressional seats during _____ elections.


MULTIPLE CHOICE

11.   The first method used for nominating candidates for public office in the United States was the
      a. direct primary.
      b. legislative caucus.
      c. national convention.
      d. closed primary.

12.   A primary in which voters choose the party for whom they wish to vote without having formally registered as a party member is called a(n)
      a. closed primary.
      b. open primary.
      c. split primary.
      d. runoff primary.

13.   Vice presidential candidates are customarily chosen by
      a. the presidential nominee.
      b. the sitting president.
      c. the leader of the party in the Senate.
      d. the leader of the party in the House.

14. A candidate who wins several primaries early in the election cycle
   a. gains the advantage of national publicity and greater popularity with the voters.
   b. can control the electoral votes in those states.
   c. gains the support of the other party candidates.
   d. generally runs out of money before the general election.

15. The law that provides for public financing of presidential elections is the
   a. Executive Branch Reform Act of 1925.
   b. Political Activities Act of 1933.
   c. Campaign Funding Act of 1950.
   d. Federal Election Campaign Act of 1974.

16. The 2002 Bipartisan Campaign Finance Law did NOT
   a. raise the amount of money that could be contributed to candidates for public office.
   b. outlaw soft money contributions to the national political parties.
   c. criminalize airing political issue-related ads on television within sixty days of an election.
   d. limit the amount of money that candidates can spend on their own campaigns.

17. The pattern of campaign contributions to candidates for the U.S. House of
   Representatives strongly favors
   a. Democratic party candidates.
   b. Republican party candidates.
   c. incumbents over challengers.
   d. challengers over incumbents.

18. Which of the following states have the greatest influence on the outcome of presidential elections?
   a. California, Texas, New York, and Florida
   b. Delaware, New Hampshire, Vermont, and Maine
   c. Minnesota, North Dakota, South Dakota, and Washington
   d. Virginia, North Carolina, South Carolina, and Georgia

19. Candidates for the Democratic party tend to stress _____ in their campaign strategy.
   a. patriotism
   b. party unity
   c. religion
   d. traditional values

20. In the early twentieth century, states adopted voter registration systems in an attempt to
   a. increase voter turnout.
   b. decrease voter turnout.
   c. simplify the process of voting.
   d. reduce voting fraud.

21. The party-column ballot encourages
   a. split-ticket voting.
   b. straight-ticket voting.
   c. winner-take-all voting.
   d. independent voting.

22. Which proposal for reforming the Electoral College would encourage the growth of minor political parties?
a. winner-take-all voting
b. single-member district plan
c. direct popular election
d. eliminating the electors but leaving the electoral vote system in place

23. A popular presidential candidate on the ballot may bring into office a number of members of his or her party. This is called the
a. surge effect.
b. coattail effect.
c. maintaining effect.
d. reinstating effect.

24. The 2002 legislation passed by Congress to improve the methods of voting in the United States provides money to help states
a. switch to an Internet-based voting system.
b. locate and register previously unregistered potential voters.
c. grant citizenship to illegal aliens for purposes of registration and voting.
d. purchase new or upgrade their old voting systems.

25. A presidential candidate must receive _____ votes to be elected by the Electoral College.
a. 538
b. 325
c. 270
d. 125

TRUE OR FALSE

26. Political parties generally favor closed primaries.
T  F

27. The main task of the national convention is to nominate the party's presidential and vice presidential candidates.
T  F

28. Participation in midterm congressional elections has traditionally been higher than in presidential elections.
T  F

29. Tax exempt 527 committees are allowed to donate money directly to political parties or candidates.
T  F

30. The Republican party regained control over Congress during the 2006 midterm elections.
T  F

## DISCUSSION, ESSAY

31. Describe how the presidential nomination process has changed over time, and identify advantages and disadvantages of different methods of choosing presidential candidates.

32. Some critics of the current process of presidential nominations favor replacing the system with a national primary. Discuss the criticisms of the current process, what the national primary would do to change the current process, and whether you feel that the national primary is the best idea for reform.

33. Briefly explain the functions of the Electoral College. Discuss the problems associated with using such a system in a democratic society and offer at least one example from recent elections.

34. Explain who votes in the United States and how that has changed over time. Also, offer reasons why those who do not vote choose not to participate and what we might do to increase turnout.

35. Explain how and why Democratic and Republican candidates use different campaign strategies. Offer examples.

## ABC NEWS/PRENTICE HALL VIDEO LIBRARY: AMERICAN GOVERNMENT

**AIR WARS**
**Originally Aired: 8/25/04**
**Program: *Nightline***
**Running Time: 9:07**

The group known as the "Swift Boat Veterans for Truth" continues to stir the 2004 presidential election. One of President Bush's election lawyers, Benjamin Ginsberg, stepped down from his role in the Bush campaign after admitting ties with the group that has been attacking John Kerry's war record. Mr. Ginsberg resigned after voluntarily disclosing his role as an advisor to both the Bush campaign and the "Swift Boat Veterans for Truth." Is this dual role a violation of federal election laws? Technically it isn't, but the appearance of a "connection" could still have political consequences. Ginsberg's admission of ties with the so-called "527 group" comes after the president has categorically denied that a connection exists between his campaign and the television ads in question. Chris Bury talks to Benjamin Ginsberg about his connection with the "Swift Boat Veterans for Truth," his decision to resign from his position as National Counsel to the Bush campaign, and what this means for the Republicans.
Both sides of the political spectrum have 527 groups—for example, you may have heard of the liberal Moveon.org or conservative Club for Growth. What's important to note is that a significant amount more—$136 million more—has been raised by Democratic-tied groups over the Republican-tied groups.

On this program, ABC's Jake Tapper will help us understand these groups and their impact on the 2004 election. He'll also explain the political connections on both sides to these groups.

## Critical Thinking Question

1. The Bipartisan Campaign Reform Act (BCRA) bans most forms of soft money. According to "Air Wars," a loophole in BCRA has allowed outside groups to raise and spend unlimited amounts of money supporting or attacking candidates as long as the candidate's campaign doesn't "coordinate the messages." What does this mean? Use examples from the video.

2. What is a 527 group? What are 527 groups allowed to do? What aren't they allowed to do?

3. In "Air Wars," political scientist Ken Goldstein gives a number of reasons why negative ads are so successful. Briefly discuss at least three of these reasons.

4. Are there any important campaign finance-related issues that BCRA does not address? Briefly discuss one or two of these issues and any efforts to address them independently.

# CHAPTER 7
# CONGRESS

## CHAPTER OVERVIEW

Chapter 7 describes the organization and structure of Congress and the procedures used by Congress to conduct its work. The chapter begins by distinguishing between the legislative and representational functions of Congress. The legislative functions of Congress are either expressly stated in the Constitution or implied by the "necessary and proper clause," which gives Congress the power to make laws that are required to execute the powers that are expressly stated in the Constitution. The representation function of members of Congress is to act on behalf of the members of their states or congressional districts. Representation takes two basic forms. The first is the promotion of policies that are favorable to a legislator's constituents. The second is referred to as casework, which involves nonlegislative activities that benefit individuals or groups in a legislator's state or congressional district.

The chapter describes the process of reapportionment, whereby seats in the House of Representatives are allocated among the states on the basis of population. The chapter also identifies similarities and differences between the House and Senate and discusses the characteristics of members of Congress. The chapter also describes the leadership structure of the two houses of Congress and the committee system. It is in committees and subcommittees that most of the work of Congress is conducted. Chapter 7 concludes with a discussion of how legislation is introduced in Congress and the process by which introduced bills either succeed or fail to become law.

## LEARNING OBJECTIVES

1. Outline the major legislative and representative functions of Congress.
2. Define the leadership offices, roles, and functions in the House of Representatives and the Senate.
3. Explain the major types of congressional committees, and discuss how the committee system operates in each house.
4. Describe the process for passing legislation in Congress.
5. Define gerrymandering and discuss the process whereby the boundary lines for congressional districts are drawn and the requirements that must be met.

## CHAPTER OUTLINE

I. The functions of Congress
   A. Legislative functions: Expressed powers
      1. Taxing and spending (authorizations/appropriations)
      2. The budget process (proposed federal budget in 2003 was $2.1 trillion)
      3. Interstate commerce
      4. Foreign affairs and treaties (the September 11 attacks and Iraq examples)
   B. Legislative functions: Implied powers

C. Representation
    1. Policy representation
    2. Service
D. Other constitutional functions
    1. Watchdog and oversight functions
    2. Appointments
    3. Electoral functions
    4. Vice presidential nominations and presidential disability
    5. Impeachment (House brings charges; Senate acts as jury)
    6. Amendments to the Constitution
    7. Disciplining and expelling members (James A. Traficant)

II.    The congressional district
    A. Reapportionment ("one person, one vote")
    B. Gerrymandering
    C. Race cannot be used as a basis for the districting
    D. States in South/West helped by 2000 census; East/West suffered declines

III.    The two houses: Similarities and differences
    A. Similarities
        1. Equal partners in lawmaking
        2. The majority party elects the leadership
        3. The majority party controls committees
        4. Committee chairs are from the majority party
    B. Differences
        1. Size
        2. Style
        3. Rules
        4. Terms of office
        5. Political outlook of members

IV.    The members of Congress
    A. Upper middle class
    B. College-educated with backgrounds in law, business, and public service or politics
    C. Few women and minorities
        1. In 110th Congress, 16 women in the Senate
        2. In 110th Congress, 42 African Americans and 27 Hispanics in the House

V.    Congressional leadership
    A. The Speaker of the House
    B. Senate leadership
        1. President of the Senate
        2. President Pro Tempore
    C. The majority leaders
        1. Senate majority leader
        2. House majority leader
    D. Minority leaders and floor whips
        1. Minority leaders
        2. Whips

VI.    The committee system
    A. Types of committees
        1. Standing committees (19 in House, 17 in Senate)
        2. Select committees (often used for oversight purposes)

        3. Joint committees

        4. Conference committees

    B. Committee assignments

    C. Committee chairs

    D. The major committees

    E. The legislative bureaucracy

        1. Member's staff aides

        2. Committee staff aides

VII. The legislative process

    A. The introduction of a bill

    B. The committee stage

    C. The calendar

    D. Floor procedure

        1. In the House

        2. In the Senate

        3. Filibusters

    E. Presidential approval or disapproval

## CHAPTER SUMMARY

The U.S. system of government cannot be understood without a comprehensive understanding of Congress. Congress is both a legislative and representative body. Congress enacts legislation for the entire nation, but each member of Congress represents the people of a specific state or congressional district.

Congress has explicit constitutional powers to pass tax laws, which raise money, and appropriations laws, which determine how the money is spent. In 1974, Congress passed the Budget and Impoundment Control Act to create a new procedure for establishing the annual budget for the nation. This act created budget committees in both houses of Congress, limited the president's power to impound funds, and established a new schedule for the budget process and the enactment of all tax, authorization, and appropriations legislation.

Congress also has broad expressed constitutional powers to regulate interstate and international commerce, declare war, and raise and support an army and navy. The president has the power to negotiate treaties with foreign nations, but two-thirds of the Senate must approve a treaty for it to take effect.

Constitutional scholars have described the Constitution as inviting a struggle over the conduct of foreign policy between the president and Congress. The War Powers Resolution of 1973 is the most important attempt by Congress to limit the president's power to make war. In the 1980s and 1990s, Congress retreated from the assertive position of the War Powers Resolution and offered little opposition to presidential decisions concerning the use of military force. Additionally, the September 11 attacks and the subsequent military actions against terrorism saw Congress generally supporting presidential requests for greater homeland and overseas security.

In addition to the powers that the Constitution explicitly assigns to Congress, Article I, Section 8, of the Constitution concludes by granting implied powers to allow Congress to do all things "necessary and proper" to carry out its constitutional duties.

In fulfilling the representation function of Congress, members of Congress engage in two distinct types of activities: policy representation and service. Policy representation involves attempting to pass legislation on behalf of a member's constituents. Service involves responding to requests from individuals and groups from a member's constituency, such as following up on a tardy tax refund for an individual constituent or inquiring after payment to a company that does business with the government within a member's state or district.

Congress also undertakes many other constitutional functions, including watchdog and oversight functions, consideration of amendments to the Constitution, and acceptance or rejection of presidential nominees to the Supreme Court and the executive branch.

The Constitution provides that House seats shall be assigned on the basis of population. The resulting task of reapportionment involves the re-drawing of congressional district boundaries, where necessary, to reflect changes in population size. Reapportionment is performed every ten years, based on the results of the national census. The boundaries of congressional districts within each state are determined by the state legislatures.

Until the 1960s, rural and small-town interests dominated state legislatures. As a result, population shifts from rural areas and small towns to cities and suburbs were not reflected in the process of reapportionment, and citizens living in urban areas were underrepresented in the House of Representatives. In 1964, the issue of unequal representation reached the Supreme Court in the case of *Wesberry* v. *Sanders*. The Supreme Court applied the principle of one person, one vote to congressional elections, requiring that states draw district boundaries to more accurately reflect the distribution of population within a state.

State legislatures may still take political considerations into account when drawing congressional district lines. The practice known as gerrymandering refers to the drawing of congressional district lines to benefit the majority party in the state legislature. In redistricting following the 1990 census, a number of states created districts in which African Americans and Hispanics were in the majority. The constitutionality of using race as a factor in drawing district lines, even if to advantage minority groups, was challenged. In response, the Supreme Court declared congressional districts drawn with race as a predominant factor to be unconstitutional, but that race could be a secondary factor if the primary motivation in districting is political.

The House and Senate are equal partners in the legislative process, but they also differ in some respects. The House is larger, more formal, and has more complex rules that govern the legislative process. House members give more attention to local issues of concern to their congressional district, whereas senators have a more diverse constituency and have to consider a broader range of concerns. Elections for the House occur at two-year intervals, whereas senators have a six-year term. This requires House members to pay greater attention to campaigning.

Members of Congress do not constitute a representative sample of the entire U.S. population, but rather are more likely to come from the upper middle class. Most members of Congress have careers in professions such as law, banking, education, or business. Women and racial minorities are also underrepresented in Congress, although their numbers are increasing.

The highest position of leadership in the House is the Speaker of the House, who is elected by the entire chamber. The power of the Speaker of the House has changed over time, and although the Speaker's position remains powerful, it was greater in the past. The House majority leader is second in command to the Speaker. In the Senate, leadership includes the President of the Senate, the President *Pro Tempore*, and the Senate majority leader. No position of leadership in the Senate has ever been as powerful as the Speaker of the House. Both the House and Senate elect minority leaders and majority and minority whips. The Speaker of the House and the majority leaders and whips are elected by the majority party in Congress, and the minority leaders and whips are elected by the minority party.

Most of the actual work of Congress is done in committees, and the most important committees in Congress are the permanent, or standing, committees. The standing committees are typically divided into subcommittees. Select or special committees are formed to consider particular issues or new areas of legislation, and joint committees are formed to deal with concerns that require coordination between the two houses. Conference committees are joint committees that work out a compromise when the two chambers pass different versions of a bill. The majority party holds a majority of seats on committees and subcommittees, and committee chairs and subcommittee chairs are chosen by the majority party.

Until the 1970s, chairs of standing committees had broad powers and were chosen on the basis of seniority, whereby the majority party member with the longest continuous service on a committee was selected as chair. A series of reforms in the 1970s reduced the powers of committee chairs, increased the powers of committee members, and modified the seniority system. As a result of these reforms, new members of Congress are in a much better position to influence the legislative process than they were in the past.

The legislative process begins with public awareness of an issue. As issues become more prominent, they are more likely to be placed on the policy agenda, and members of Congress often introduce bills to address these issues. Once a bill is introduced, it is assigned to a committee. If approved, it goes to the full House or Senate, where floor debate occurs on the bill and it is subject to amendment. If a bill successfully passes both houses, it is sent to the president. The president can sign the bill, in which case it becomes law. Alternately, the president can veto the bill and send it back to Congress. At this point, Congress can override the veto by a two-thirds vote in each house.

In recent decades, divided government—in which Congress and the executive are controlled by different political parties—has become common. Divided government is accompanied by the image of "gridlock," or a government unable to agree on important policy concerns facing the nation. Whether divided government is actually associated with gridlock is called into question by research on the issue. There is evidence, however, that divided government is a conscious choice of voters who do not wish to give either political party the sole power to control public policy.

## KEY TERMS

| | |
|---|---|
| appropriations | oversight |
| authorization | policy agenda |
| calendar | President of the Senate |
| casework | President *Pro Tempore* |
| cloture vote | public hearings |
| conference committees | reapportionment |
| discharge petition | rule |
| filibuster | select committees |
| gerrymandering | Senate majority leader |
| House majority leader | seniority system |
| impeachment | Speaker of the House |
| implied powers | standing committees |
| joint committees | unanimous consent agreements |
| minority leaders | veto |
| override | whips |

# PRACTICE EXERCISES

## FILL IN THE BLANKS

1. Taxes are used to both raise money and _____ the economy.

2. Congress often passes stopgap spending bills to keep federal agencies running when regular spending bills aren't enacted by the October 1 deadline. These are called _____ _____.

3. The Constitution requires that treaties made by the president with other nations must receive the advice and consent of two-thirds of the _____.

4. Every ten years, there is a redrawing of legislative district lines on the basis of new population information supplied by the U.S. Census Bureau. This task is called _____.

5. The division of congressional districts so as to give advantage to the majority party is called _____.

6. The Senate's 2002 investigation into the September 11 attacks illustrates the _____ function of Congress.

7. House standing committees average about forty members, and each member of the House serves on an average of _____ committees and subcommittees.

8. Joint committees that are formed to establish a compromise between House and Senate versions of the same bill are called _____ committees.

9. A _____ is when one or more Senators try to keep legislation from coming to vote by speaking continually.

10. To override a presidential veto, _____ of each house of Congress must vote in favor of a vetoed bill.

## MULTIPLE CHOICE

11. The process by which Congress establishes specific programs and sets limits on the amount of money that may be spent on these programs is called
    a. revenue enhancement.
    b. taxation.
    c. authorization.
    d. appropriation.

12. The constitutional basis for much of the legislation that Congress has passed to control and regulate the economy is the
    a. commerce clause.
    b. Economic Powers Resolution.
    c. reserved powers clause.
    d. oversight clause.

13. The _____ requires the president to end the use of military force within 60 days unless Congress declares war or agrees to the continued use of the U.S. armed forces in combat situations.
    a. Congressional Oversight Act
    b. USA PATRIOT Act
    c. War Preventions Act
    d. War Powers Resolution

14. The president's nominations to the Supreme Court must be approved by
    a. the Executive Cabinet.
    b. the Chief Justice of the Supreme Court.
    c. the Senate.
    d. the House of Representatives.

15. The power to impeach, or to bring formal charges against the president or another high official, is held by
    a. the Supreme Court.
    b. the executive cabinet.
    c. the Senate.
    d. the House of Representatives.

16. In the process of reapportionment, the Supreme Court has declared which of the following to be unconstitutional?
    a. racial gerrymandering, whereby race is the predominant factor in drawing boundaries for a congressional district
    b. political gerrymandering, whereby partisan or other political interests are the predominant factor in drawing the boundaries for a congressional district
    c. any type of gerrymandering, regardless of the purpose for the gerrymander
    d. using the criteria of one person, one vote as the predominant factor in drawing the boundaries for a congressional district

17. In the case of a tie vote in the Senate, to whom does the Constitution give the power to vote to break the tie?
    a. the president
    b. the vice president
    c. the Speaker of the House
    d. the Senate majority leader

18. The House and Senate are similar in that
    a. both have 435 members.
    b. both have the same set of rules and procedures.
    c. committees are controlled by the majority party.
    d. two-year election intervals require constant attention to campaigning.

19. Eastern and Midwestern states lost House seats to Southern and Western states during the _____ that followed the 2000 census; this trend is expected to continue through the next several decades.
    a. reapportionment
    b. gerrymandering
    c. redistricting
    d. reforms

20. Created in 1795, the _____ is the oldest standing committee in the House and has the widest jurisdiction of any congressional committee.
    a. House Rules Committee
    b. House Ways and Means Committee
    c. House Committee on Energy and Commerce
    d. House Committee on Financial Services

21. Although a member of Congress must introduce a bill, most major items of legislation originate
    a. with interest groups.
    b. in the media.
    c. with popular referendum.
    d. in the executive branch.

22. As a result of reforms carried out in the 1970s,
    a. the power of committee chairs has been greatly increased.
    b. newly elected members of Congress may have more influence on the legislative process.
    c. all committee chairs are appointed on the basis of the seniority system.
    d. the majority party must allow members of the minority party to chair one or more of the important standing committees.

23. The House Ways and Means Committee deals with issues of
    a. foreign policy.
    b. agriculture.
    c. banking and financial services.
    d. taxation and tariffs.

24. Currently, the vote required to end a filibuster in the Senate by cloture is
    a. a simple majority of the entire Senate membership.
    b. a two-thirds majority of the entire Senate membership.
    c. a two-thirds majority of those senators present at the time of the vote.
    d. a three-fifths majority of the entire Senate.

25. Bills are considered on the floor of the Senate either in the order they appear on the Senate calendar or under a
    a. discharge petition.
    b. public hearing.
    c. unanimous consent agreement.
    d. cloture vote.

TRUE OR FALSE

26. Congressional power to impeach and convict was used unsuccessfully against President Nixon.
T  F

27. Only a small number of the bills that are introduced to Congress successfully become law.
T  F

28. Bills may only be introduced in the House of Representatives.
T  F

29. In the House, discharge petitions are used to take a bill out of the jurisdiction of a committee.
T  F

30. A large majority of presidential vetoes are overridden successfully by both houses of Congress.
T  F

DISCUSSION, ESSAY

31. One important function of members of Congress is to represent the people of their particular district or state. Identify and describe the two basic forms of this representation.

32. Identify and describe the constitutional functions of Congress. Discuss historical examples of each of these.

33. Describe the committee system and its importance to the central operation of Congress. Include examples of major standing committees and discuss their impact on the passage and formulation of legislation.

34. List and describe several similarities and differences between the House of Representatives and the Senate.

35. Describe the process by which a bill becomes a law. What are the obstacles to successful enactment of a bill into law?

**ABC NEWS/PRENTICE HALL VIDEO LIBRARY: AMERICAN GOVERNMENT**

**PRICE OF VICTORY**
**Originally Aired: 3/25/04**
**Program:** *Nightline*
**Running Time: 14:34**

It was meant to be a victory that could be savored all the way through the 2004 election. When the president signed the Medicare bill into law last December, it was a landmark event. This bill had managed to achieve what seniors had been demanding for years—prescription drug coverage. That's definitely something to celebrate. Well, a funny thing happened on the way to the bill becoming law: accusations of bribery, lying, intimidation, political shenanigans—it has become quite a Washington drama. A bureaucrat who you probably wouldn't normally hear about testified on Capitol Hill. Richard Foster is the chief actuary of the Medicare program and he says that his boss threatened to fire him if he publicized his estimates of how much the Medicare bill would actually cost. His boss happens to be a political appointee. The bill that passed had a cost estimate of around $400 billion. Foster's estimate—$534 billion—became public a month after the signing of the bill. Needless to say, people are furious, including Republicans who now say if they knew then what they know now, they would not have voted for the bill.

Then there is that story of the endless vote in the House—a fifteen-minute roll call that stayed open for three hours. A lot of arm-twisting occurred that night, including allegations that retiring Congressman Nick Smith (R-Michigan) was told that if he voted for the bill his son would get $100,000 worth of help for his upcoming congressional race. Smith voted against the bill but there is another investigation of this allegation.

There are some people who roll their eyes at the very thought of the congressional process. But this is a dramatic one. People are really emotional about it, as you will see in this program.

### Critical Thinking Questions

1. In "Price of Victory," of what does Medicare actuary Richard Foster accuse the administration?

2. In the process of passing the 2003 Medicare bill, what was unusual in regard to the timing of the vote?

3. In "Price of Victory," of what does Representative Nick Smith accuse the House leadership?

4. Your text describes the process by which bills become laws. How does the process in the text differ from the process in the video?

# CHAPTER 8
## THE CHIEF EXECUTIVE

### CHAPTER OVERVIEW

Chapter 8 examines the constitutional foundations of the office of the president, the powers of the executive, and the limits on executive power. The chapter also identifies how the presidency is a product of the individuals who have held office and the way that these individuals have exercised power.

The chapter begins by reviewing constitutional guidelines for the selection and removal of the president. These include the eligibility requirements for presidents, specifications for the transfer of presidential duties in the case of the death or disability, and the process by which a president may be impeached and removed.

The chapter then describes the roles and powers of the president, which include both constitutional roles and powers and those arising from congressional legislation, and precedents set by earlier presidents. The chapter also reviews the limits on the power of the executive, which include judicial review, the Budget and Impoundment Control Act, the bureaucracy, the media, and public opinion.

The Constitution establishes the presidency as a one-person office and specifies both the formal powers and limits on the powers of the presidency. Despite the growth of the executive branch in the twentieth century, the presidency effectively remains a one-person office, and the personal dimension of the executive has been an important influence on the power and effectiveness of individual presidents.

Chapter 8 concludes with a discussion of the office of the vice president and how recent presidents have attempted to give more importance to that office.

### LEARNING OBJECTIVES

1. Outline the legal requirements for a person to serve as president of the United States.
2. Discuss the similarities and differences between a treaty and an executive agreement, explaining how and why each is used.
3. Assess the changing nature of presidential power.
4. Discuss the nature of checks and balances between the presidency and the Congress.
5. Explain the origins of the War Powers Act and assess its effectiveness.
6. List and define the four categories of presidential character.
7. Explain the problems associated with presidential succession and consider how the Constitution approaches this problem.

### CHAPTER OUTLINE

I. Selection and removal of the president
   A. Who may become president?
   B. Succession and disability
   C. Impeachment and removal
II. The president's roles and powers
   A. Chief of state

B. Roles related to foreign affairs
   1. Chief diplomat
   2. Treaties and executive agreements
   3. Formulation of foreign policy
   4. World leader
C. Commander in chief
D. Chief administrator
E. Chief legislator
   1. The veto power
   2. The pardon power
F. Party leader
G. National opinion leader
H. Manager of the economy

III.   Limits on the president's powers
A. Judicial review
B. The War Powers Resolution
C. The Budget and Impoundment Control Act
D. The bureaucracy
E. The media
F. Public opinion

IV.   The personal dimension
A. Beliefs, motivation, skills
B. Presidential character

V.   The vice president
A. Constitutional provisions
B. Selection
C. Duties and assignments
D. Dick Cheney/George W. Bush

## CHAPTER SUMMARY

Article II of the Constitution begins with the statement that "the executive power shall be vested in a President of the United States." The Constitution goes on to specify that the president must have lived in the United States at least 14 years, must be at least 35 years old, and must have been born either in the United States or to parents who are U.S. citizens. Article II of the Constitution provides that if the president cannot discharge his duties, the vice president assumes the full powers of the president. Based on ambiguities in the statement of succession in Article II, the Twenty-fifth Amendment was ratified in 1967. This amendment provides detailed provisions for the transfer of power and for the process to be followed in the case of presidential disability, including situations in which the president is either unwilling or unable to declare disability. This amendment also provides for the appointment of a vice president if that office becomes vacant.

The Constitution provides the power to impeach and remove the president from power in cases of "Treason, Bribery, or other high Crimes and Misdemeanors." The House of Representatives is charged with determining whether there are sufficient grounds to warrant impeachment, and the president is impeached on the basis of a majority vote in the House. Following impeachment, the Senate serves as a court, conducting a trial to determine the veracity of the charges of impeachment. The president is removed from office if two-thirds of all senators present vote in favor of conviction on the charges of impeachment. Presidents Andrew Johnson and Bill Clinton are the only presidents who have been impeached by the House, and neither Johnson nor Clinton was convicted by the Senate.

The roles and powers of the president are a mixture of constitutionally specified tasks and roles and powers that have arisen from congressional legislation or by custom and precedent. The roles of chief of state, chief diplomat, commander in chief of the armed forces (note President George W. Bush's leadership after the September 11 attacks and his direction of U.S. military forces in Afghanistan and Iraq), chief administrator, and chief legislator have arisen based on specifications in the Constitution. The power to negotiate treaties, appoint all U.S. ambassadors and other high-ranking officials, advise the Congress on the state of the nation, veto legislation, and grant reprieves and pardons are among those executive powers granted by the Constitution. On the other hand, the president's roles as world leader, leader of his or her political party, national opinion leader, and manager of the economy have arisen over time based on precedent and custom.

The Constitution provides the basis for an executive office that has grown significantly in influence and power. Yet the framers of the Constitution also provided important checks on presidential power. Through the process of judicial review, the Supreme Court has the right to declare actions taken by the president to be unconstitutional. The Supreme Court has been reluctant to challenge the legality of a president's actions in times of war, but it has been more willing to curb presidential power in the realm of domestic policy. Supreme Court decisions were instrumental in the events that led to the resignation of President Nixon and the impeachment of President Clinton.

Presidential power is also checked by Congress. Congress shares control of American military policy through its power to appropriate money for military purposes and its power to declare war. Congress passed the War Powers Resolution in 1973 in an attempt to further limit the president's military power. The president's appointment powers and power to negotiate treaties are checked by the necessity of gaining Senate approval. Other controls on presidential power are not specified in the Constitution, but have arisen over time. These include bureaucratic resistance to change, the news media, and public opinion.

The powers of the president are also influenced by each president's personal qualities. Based on personal views concerning the appropriate power of the executive, presidents may be classified as either "weak" or "strong." Weak presidents consciously limit their power as chief executive, whereas strong presidents believe that presidential power should be extended according to need and should be limited only by the system of checks and balances. Presidents also differ in terms of motivation, skill, and other characteristics. Political scientist James David Barber developed a theory to analyze the relationship between presidential character and politics.

Created by the framers of the Constitution as an afterthought, the office of vice president is relatively weak with ambiguous duties. Recent presidents have attempted to give their vice presidents more important assignments. Although the office remains weak, it has the potential to become very important in the case of disability or death of the president. Dick Cheney has been a very influential vice president during the George W. Bush administration.

## KEY TERMS

| | |
|---|---|
| executive agreement | pocket veto |
| impeachment | treaty |
| line item veto | veto |

# PRACTICE EXERCISES

## FILL IN THE BLANKS

1. The office of the presidency is established in Article _____ of the Constitution.

2. The Constitution gives the power to impeach to the _____.

3. The Constitution gives the power to convict and remove an impeached official from office to the _____.

4. Only two presidents have been impeached: _____ _____ and _____ _____. None have been convicted and removed.

5. A treaty requires the advice and consent of two-thirds of the _____ before it can be signed by the president and take effect.

6. An understanding between the president and the chief executive of a foreign nation that does not require the advice and consent of the Senate is called a(n)_____ _____.

7. A president may refuse to sign a legislative bill, and if Congress adjourns within ten days, the bill fails to become law. This is known as a(n) _____ _____.

8. The ability to mark out portions of a bill and sign it into law after the bill has passed the legislature is a power enjoyed by many state governors, but denied to the president. This is called a _____ _____ _____.

9. The authority to refuse to spend money that has been appropriated by Congress is known as _____. This practice was severely limited with the 1974 Budget and Impoundment Control Act.

10. The news media restrains the power of government by continually examining public officials and governmental action. The power of the news media was demonstrated in its coverage of the Nixon scandal, _____, which ultimately led to Nixon's resignation.


## MULTIPLE CHOICE

11. Based on provisions in the Twenty-fifth Amendment, if a president becomes disabled, who becomes acting president?
    a. the Speaker of the House
    b. the Secretary of State
    c. the Attorney General
    d. the vice president

12. The president's power to grant diplomatic recognition to a country stems from the power to
    a. send and receive ambassadors.
    b. appoint commanders.
    c. negotiate treaties.
    d. declare war.

13. When the Senate takes no action on a treaty proposed by the president, the treaty
    a. takes effect on the basis of the president's signature alone.
    b. requires a two-thirds majority vote of support in the House before it can take effect.
    c. requires a majority vote of support from the National Security Council before it can take effect.
    d. is prevented from taking effect.

14. Senators have criticized executive agreements as a means of bypassing the Senate's constitutional right to give advice and consent to international agreements. The Supreme Court has found that executive agreements
    a. are unconstitutional.
    b. have the same legal force as treaties.
    c. may only be used in negotiations to end a war.
    d. may only be used in trade negotiations.

15. The Constitution says nothing about how treaties can or should be terminated, yet, historically, the _____ has been allowed to decide when a treaty has outlived its usefulness.
    a. House.
    b. president.
    c. Congress (both House and Senate).
    d. Senate.

16. Acting as _____ _____, modern presidents have become increasingly involved in direct negotiation with the heads of foreign governments.
    a. chief legislator
    b. chief administrator
    c. party leader
    d. chief diplomat

17. The president's power to grant reprieves and pardons is limited by
    a. an inability to grant reprieves or pardons in cases of impeachment.
    b. a required two-thirds vote of approval from the Senate.
    c. a required majority vote of approval from the Supreme Court.
    d. the required approval of the chief justice of the Supreme Court.

18. The presidential speech that is called for by the Constitution and consists of a general statement of policy is known as the
    a. National Budget message.
    b. State of the Union address.
    c. Annual Economic Report.
    d. Congressional Midterm Report.

19. Following the September 11 attacks on the U.S., the president was granted broad, new powers in the area of surveillance, money laundering, and immigration with the _____ _____.
   a. USA PATRIOT Act.
   b. War Powers Resolution.
   c. Sedition Act.
   d. Terrorist Control Act.

20. The president is responsible for the management of the agencies and departments which serve the federal government. This responsibility illustrates the president's role as
   a. world leader.
   b. chief legislator.
   c. party leader.
   d. chief administrator.

21. Which president is known for his "fireside chats" during the Great Depression of the 1930s?
   a. Franklin Roosevelt
   b. Theodore Roosevelt
   c. Herbert Hoover
   d. Harry Truman

22. Which president is often referred to as "the great communicator"?
   a. Ronald Reagan
   b. Richard Nixon
   c. Herbert Hoover
   d. Franklin Roosevelt

23. Which of the following is *not* one of the three main presidential communications concerned with legislative matters?
   a. the Executive Priorities Report
   b. the State of the Union Address
   c. the National Budget message
   d. the Annual Economic Report

24. All presidential actions are subject to _____ _____ to ensure that they are constitutional.
   a. peer scrutiny
   b. judicial review
   c. congressional approval
   d. open review

25. The Supreme Court has been reluctant to declare presidential actions illegal in situations of
   a. impeachment.
   b. economic prosperity.
   c. war.
   d. conflict between the president and the chief justice of the Supreme Court.

TRUE OR FALSE

26. If the president dies or is removed from office, the vice president assumes the office of the president, and the Speaker of the House assumes the office of the vice president.
T  F

27. Richard Nixon is the only president to be both impeached by the House and convicted and removed from office by the Senate.
T  F

28. Executive agreements are far more common than treaties.
T  F

29. The presidential role as a leader of his or her political party is one of the roles assigned to the president by the Constitution.
T  F

30. The power of the executive branch has dramatically increased over the course of U.S. history.
T  F

DISCUSSION, ESSAY

31. Identify the roles and powers of the president, and distinguish between those that are specified in the Constitution and those that have developed on the basis of custom and precedent.

32. Explain the constitutional provision for the transfer of presidential duties in the event of death, resignation, or disability.

33. Discuss the procedure for impeachment and removal of a president of the United States. Discuss President Bill Clinton's impeachment and whether you believe that impeachment was justified. Additionally, discuss whether there was sufficient cause for him to have been convicted and/or removed from office.

34. Define "commander in chief" and the president's responsibility and authority in this role. Include a discussion of George W. Bush's actions as commander in chief during the War in Iraq and the war on terrorism sparked by the September 11 attacks.

35. Discuss James D. Barber's theory of presidential character and offer presidential examples of each type. Explain why you selected your examples, which type Barber feels we should avoid, and why.

# CHAPTER 9
## THE FEDERAL BUREAUCRACY

## CHAPTER OVERVIEW

Chapter 9 begins with a description of the nature of bureaucracies and the obstacles to change in the federal bureaucracy. The chapter goes on to describe how the federal bureaucracy is organized and discusses both the powers of and the restraints on the bureaucracy. The agencies that comprise a bureaucracy, line agencies and staff agencies, are identified and compared. The chapter then provides an overview of the line and staff agencies within the U.S. federal government and discusses how these agencies have changed over time.

The chapter also includes a discussion of the size of the bureaucracy as well as a description of the process of staffing the federal bureaucracy. The chapter identifies political executives as high-level government employees who hold important policy-making positions in government and are appointed by the president and confirmed by the Senate. Sources of power within the federal bureaucracy, including size, expertise, relationships with congressional committees and interest groups, and the delegation by Congress of broad powers to the executive branch and independent regulatory commissions, are also discussed.

Chapter 9 concludes by identifying and describing the federal bureaucracy, including restraints imposed by the president, Congress, the judiciary, employees, the media, and private groups that may serve to limit the actions of the bureaucracy. Despite criticism of the bureaucracy, it seems unlikely that significant change will occur in the foreseeable future.

## LEARNING OBJECTIVES

1. Describe the organization of the federal bureaucracy.
2. Discuss the evolution of the cabinet departments over time and assess the major functions of the cabinet secretaries.
3. Assess the mechanisms whereby the civil service system evaluates persons fairly for federal jobs or for promotions.
4. Explain the sources of and restraints on bureaucratic power in the federal government.
5. Describe how the Executive Office of the President operates, assessing the functions and services provided by its various elements.

## CHAPTER OUTLINE

I. The organization of the executive branch
   A. Line agencies
      1. The executive departments
      2. Agencies
      3. Corporations
      4. Independent regulatory commissions
      5. Independent central services and control agencies

B. Staff agencies
    1. The cabinet
    2. The Executive Office of the President
       a. The White House Office
       b. The Office of Management and Budget
       c. The Council of Economic Advisers
       d. The National Security Council

II.    The federal bureaucrats
   A. The size of the bureaucracy
   B. Who are the bureaucrats?
      1. The spoils system
      2. The merit system
      3. Classification
      4. Political executives

III.   Sources of bureaucratic power
   A. Size
   B. Expertise
   C. The agency/committee/interest group triangle
   D. Delegation of power by Congress

IV.   Restraints on the bureaucracy
   A. The powers of the president
      1. Appointment power
      2. Removal powers
      3. Power to reorganize
      4. The president's leadership role
   B. The powers of Congress
      1. Budgetary powers
      2. Organizational powers
      3. Lawmaking powers
      4. Passage of legislation
        a. The Freedom of Information Act of 1966
        b. Congressional Budget and Impoundment Control Act of 1974
      5. Legislative oversight
   C. Judicial review
   D. Whistleblowers
   E. Other restraints
      1. News media
      2. Private groups
      3. Bureaucratic internal competition
      4. Bureaucratic values
      5. Deregulation

# CHAPTER SUMMARY

An ideal bureaucracy successfully organizes people to achieve a goal in an efficient and effective manner. In reality, however, the federal bureaucracy is associated with problems of red tape and a lack of responsiveness.

Under the Clinton administration, Vice President Al Gore conducted a study to determine how the federal bureaucracy could be changed to become more efficient and effective. The results of this study were published in what came to be known as the Gore Report, which called for a reduction in red tape, greater emphasis on customer service, more power for lower-level employees, and overall cuts in spending. Although these types of reform have been suggested in earlier study-based reports, there are significant obstacles to changing the federal bureaucracy. For instance, both Congress and the president wish to respond to the demands of their constituencies, yet meeting these demands often involves the creation of more bureaucracy.

The executive branch, like any bureaucracy, is divided into line and staff agencies. The line agencies are designed to carry out government policies. In the federal bureaucracy, there are currently fifteen executive departments: State, Treasury, Defense, Justice, Interior, Agriculture, Commerce, Labor, Health and Human Services, Housing and Urban Development, Transportation, Energy, Education, Veterans Affairs, and Homeland Security. Each department is headed by a secretary, who is a member of the president's cabinet. The fifteen departments are similar in organization, but they differ greatly in size and function. Staff agencies do not carry out policy, rather they gather information and make it available to the president. In the executive branch, the main staff agency is the Executive Office of the President and, to a lesser degree, the cabinet.

Over the course of U.S. history, the executive branch has grown in both numbers of employees and complexity, as agencies and bureaus have been added or reorganized. In George Washington's first administration in 1790, there were approximately 1,000 employees in the executive branch of government. As of 2007, the number of people employed in the executive bureaucracy was 2,700,000. This number was actually a reduction since the late 1980s, resulting primarily from cuts in the Department of Defense following the end of the Cold War.

The process by which government employees are chosen has also changed over time. Until the late 1800s, government jobs were allocated on the basis of the spoils system, from the saying "to the winner go the spoils." Under the spoils systems, government jobs were awarded to political supporters and friends of the winning candidate. There were advantages to the spoils system, but it also encouraged the development of new jobs, whether necessary or not, and often resulted in the hiring of people unqualified for their positions. The 1883 Pendleton Act ended the spoils system in the federal government and replaced it with a merit system, in which individuals compete for jobs and take exams to ensure that they are qualified for their jobs. There are now fewer than 6,000 jobs in the federal government that are not covered by the merit system. More than half of these jobs are high-level policy-making positions in government and are appointed by the president.

The federal bureaucracy is often referred to as the "fourth branch of government." The bureaucracy is responsible for implementing governmental policies and programs, which gives it a great deal of power. Specific sources of bureaucratic power include size, expertise, "iron triangles," and the delegation of powers by Congress.

There are also restraints on bureaucratic power. These include presidential appointment and removal powers, as well as the president's power to reorganize the executive branch. The president can also use his leadership ability to guide the bureaucracy. Congress has several ways to limit bureaucratic power as well, including congressional control of agency budgets and authority. Since the 1970s, the powers of some agencies have been reduced through deregulation, which involves the repeal of regulatory legislation. The Freedom of Information Act, exercise of the legislative oversight function, judicial review, whistleblowers, and the news media also provide significant restraints on the bureaucracy.

## KEY TERMS

agencies

bureaucracy

bureaus

cabinet

civil service

departments

deregulation

field services

government corporations

impoundment

independent regulatory commissions

line agencies

merit system

oversight

political executives

removal power

senatorial courtesy

spoils system

staff agency

whistleblower

## PRACTICE EXERCISES

### FILL IN THE BLANKS

1. Within any bureaucracy, each department or agency falls into one of two broad categories, either _____ or _____.

2. The head of an executive department has the title of _____, and is a member of the president's cabinet.

3. Federal _____ are formed when their function is too specific, or limited, to warrant the creation of a department.

4. Government _____ combine certain aspects of the private and public sectors to provide services to the public. Most notably, these organizations are subject to some government oversight but are intended to be financially self-supporting.

5. The process of hiring government employees on the basis of their support for the winning candidate is the _____ system.

6. The process of hiring government employees on the basis of their qualifications and test scores is called a _____ system.

7. The president's _____ heads the White House Office and controls access to the president, among other duties.

8. The mutually beneficial relationship that develops among a government agency, a congressional committee, and a special interest group is called an _____ _____.

9. Government employees who disclose government fraud and waste are known as _____.

10. Many refer to the federal bureaucracy as the "_____ branch of government" because of its size and discretion in carrying out policies and programs.


MULTIPLE CHOICE

11. The most recent study on how the federal bureaucracy functions and what could be done to improve it is the
    a. Gore Report.
    b. Wilson Report.
    c. Clinton Report.
    d. Bush Report.

12. Agencies that gather information and make it available to the president are called
    a. departments.
    b. line agencies.
    c. staff agencies.
    d. commissions.

13. The tasks performed by local Social Security or Internal Revenue Service offices are called
    a. agency work.
    b. civil service.
    c. field services.
    d. agency services.

14. The majority of a bureau's employees are located in
    a. Washington, D.C.
    b. field offices.
    c. New York City.
    d. other nations.

15. The Federal Reserve Board has several functions; a major power is its ability to
    a. write the federal budget to ensure balanced spending.
    b. lower the cost of common goods to encourage spending.
    c. raise taxes to increase its reserves.
    d. raise and lower interest rates.

16. Among other reasons, independent regulatory commissions are created and given broad authority over certain areas of the nation's economy for the purpose of
    a. limiting the corrupting power of the private sector on government officials.
    b. enabling a specific group of elected officials to control certain private interests.
    c. freeing Congress from the task of legislating on complex aspects of the economy.
    d. shielding public officials from scrutiny regarding "back-door" agreements with private entities.

17. Many of the nation's independent regulatory commissions were created by Congress during
    a. the 1990s.
    b. the Reagan administration.
    c. the Eisenhower administration.
    d. the Franklin D. Roosevelt administration.

18. A criticism of independent regulatory commissions is that
    a. they are said to exercise executive, legislative, and judicial powers, a violation of the principle of separation of powers.
    b. they are said to have too little power.
    c. the president can remove a member of a commission at any time, even if the reason for removal is based on a policy disagreement.
    d. they are entirely free from influence by interest groups.

19. Civilian employees of the federal government are known as
    a. the civil service.
    b. political executives.
    c. executive staff.
    d. the cabinet.

20. The annual *Economic Report of the President* is prepared by the Council of _____ _____ and recommends adjustments in government spending and taxation.
    a. Budget Operations
    b. Bureaucratic Management
    c. Economic Advisers
    d. Executive Office

21. Which of the following offices is in charge of coordinating domestic, foreign, and military policies?
    a. the Office of Management and Budget
    b. the National Security Council
    c. the White House Office
    d. the Federal Reserve

22. The person typically in charge of the White House Office, who often controls access to the president is
    a. the first lady.
    b. the secretary of state.
    c. the chief of staff.
    d. the president's personal secretary.

23. Much more so than in the past (under the spoils system, for example), today's government employee is likely to view his or her position as
    a. a career.
    b. an obligation.
    c. a reward for party loyalty.
    d. a reward for ideological belief.

24. Which president is often associated with the spoils system?
    a. Ronald Reagan
    b. Franklin Roosevelt
    c. Herbert Hoover
    d. Andrew Jackson

25. The repeal of regulatory legislation by Congress is called
    a. impoundment.
    b. deregulation.
    c. patronage.
    d. standard repeal.

TRUE OR FALSE

26. The Federal Reserve System was created by the Constitution.
    T  F

27. The most serious fault of the spoils system is that it encourages the creation of new, often unnecessary, jobs and often led to the hiring of unqualified people.
    T  F

28. An important source of power for the federal bureaucracy is its expertise, leading to its ability to control information.
    T  F

29. The large size of the bureaucracy is largely due to the actions of Congress, which drafts legislation in very general terms that must then be implemented by the bureaucracy.
    T  F

30. Retaliation against whistleblowers in the federal bureaucracy is nearly impossible under the Whistleblowers Protection Act of 1989.
    T  F

DISCUSSION, ESSAY

31. Define bureaucracy and identify and describe several important features of the U.S. federal bureaucracy.

32. Is bureaucratic reform needed? Explain your answer and describe the current obstacles to bureaucratic reform.

33. Identify and describe the functions of the offices that are found in the Executive Office of the President.

34. Identify and discuss the sources of bureaucratic power.

35. Identify and describe the limitations on bureaucratic power, including the sources of those limitations.

CHAPTER 10
THE JUDICIARY

CHAPTER OVERVIEW

Chapter 10 focuses on the role of the judicial branch of government in the United States. The chapter begins with a discussion of the nature of the law and distinguishes among five basic types of law: common law, equity, statutory law, constitutional law, and administrative law. The chapter also distinguishes between criminal and civil law and identifies the United States legal system as an adversary system.

The United States has a dual court system comprised of federal and state courts. The chapter reviews the jurisdiction of federal and state courts, and identifies the U.S. Supreme Court as the final arbiter of federal law, and the highest court in each state as the final arbiter of the laws of that state. The chapter goes on to discuss the organization of state courts, and identifies the roles and procedures of different levels of federal courts, including the U.S. Supreme Court. Additionally, the chapter discusses how federal judges and U.S. Supreme Court justices are appointed and notes the increased scrutiny that judicial nominees have received in recent years. The power of judicial review, including its historical development and importance in the United States government, is also discussed.

The chapter concludes with a brief history of the Supreme Court and identifies how the predominant issues facing the judiciary have changed over time.

LEARNING OBJECTIVES

1.    List and define the five types of law.
2.    Name and describe the federal courts, and the jurisdiction of each.
3.    Define a writ of *certiorari* and assess its purpose.
4.    Describe the nomination process for federal judges and Supreme Court justices and assess the role of political interests in the nomination process.
5.    Define judicial review and explain its origins in the United States.
6.    Assess the role of the Senate in the confirmation process.
7.    Discuss the evolution of constitutional interpretation as the composition of the courts has changed over time.
8.    Identify and explain the different types of opinions that are delivered by the Supreme Court.
9.    Define *appellate jurisdiction*.

CHAPTER OUTLINE

I.    The law
      A. The five types of law
         1. Common law
         2. Equity
         3. Statutory law
         4. Constitutional law
         5. Administrative law

        B. Criminal and civil law

        C. The adversary system

        D. The role of the courts

        E. The role of the judge

II.      The dual court system

        A. Jurisdiction (Appellate and Original)

        B. The state courts

        C. The federal courts

            1. United States District Courts (92 in all)

            2. United States Courts of Appeals (13 in all)

III.     Supreme Court

        A. Oral arguments

        B. Conferences

        C. Opinions

            1. Majority

            2. Concurring

            3. Dissenting

        D. The role of the chief justice

        E. Bringing a case before the court

        F. The court's workload

IV.     Selection of federal judges

        A. Selecting judges for lower federal courts

        B. Judicial appointments, 1980-2005

        C. Appointing Supreme Court judges

        D. Confirmation and tenure

V.      The functions of the judiciary

        A. Judicial review

            1. Origins in *Marbury* v. *Madison* (1803)

            2. Criticisms

        B. Restrictions on the court

            1. Impeachment and conviction

            2. Congressional legislation

            3. Public opinion

            4. Constitutional amendments

            5. Judicial self-restraint versus judicial activism

VI.     The Supreme Court: A brief history

        A. 1800-1865

        B. 1865-1938

        C. 1938-present

# CHAPTER SUMMARY

Throughout U.S. history, citizens have held the judiciary in high esteem. Few citizens question the value and importance of an independent judiciary. The United States has a dual court system, with the federal court system and the fifty state court systems. Federal courts are responsible for many issues of federal law other than constitutional issues, but it is the role of the

Supreme Court as the final interpreter of the Constitution that puts the Supreme Court at the center of the nation's government.

To understand the judiciary, it is important to understand the nature of the law. Law may be defined as the principles and rules that are established by a government as applicable to the citizens and enforceable by the government. There are five basic types of law: common law, equity, statutory law, constitutional law, and administrative law. The law is also divided into two broad areas: criminal law, in which the government is always the plaintiff; and civil law, which usually involves disputes between private individuals or corporations.

Compared to the executive and legislative branches, the judiciary is largely passive. The judiciary cannot address issues unless they are raised in cases brought before the courts. Cases take the form of a conflict between each side of a dispute, and the truth is expected to emerge from the clash of opposing positions. As such, the U.S. judicial system is referred to as an adversary system.

Under the Constitution, federal courts may hear only "cases and controversies," and cannot issue advisory opinions. The concept of jurisdiction, which refers to the right of a court to hear a particular type of case, is central to understanding the U.S. court system. The right of jurisdiction arises from either a constitution or a legislative statute. The jurisdiction of state courts is very broad; that of federal courts is more limited. The jurisdiction of federal courts arises from either the subject matter or the nature of the parties involved in a particular case. Jurisdiction on the basis of subject matter includes all cases arising under the U.S. Constitution, federal laws, treaties, and admiralty and maritime cases. Jurisdiction arising from the nature of the parties in a particular case includes cases such as those in which the United States is a party, cases involving disputes between two or more states, or cases affecting ambassadors or other public ministers.

A court's jurisdiction may be original or appellate. Trial courts that establish the facts of a case and the law that applies to the case have original jurisdiction. Courts with appellate jurisdiction review appeals of the decisions of lower courts to decide whether the correct rule of law was applied in the case. The U.S. Supreme Court has both original and appellate jurisdiction. Cases that arise from original jurisdiction are rare, however. They are limited to cases affecting ambassadors, other public ministers and consuls, and cases in which states are the parties.

State court systems are organized in different ways, but the most important trial court in most states is a superior, or circuit, court. Most states then have an intermediate appellate court, followed by the highest appellate court in the state, usually called the supreme court. Most states also have special courts that handle family problems and courts that handle wills and estates.

There are two types of federal courts: constitutional and legislative. The major constitutional courts are the U.S. district courts, the U.S. courts of appeals, and the U.S. Supreme Court. The eighty-nine district courts (plus one each for D.C., Puerto Rico, and U.S. territories) are trial courts that hear both civil and criminal cases. The thirteen courts of appeals are exclusively appellate courts and also generally hear both criminal and civil cases. The decisions of the courts of appeals are of great importance because the Supreme Court only decides 75 to 80 cases during its term. Hence, most of the rulings by the courts of appeals will not be reviewed and thus will become the law of the land. The U.S. Supreme Court is the nation's highest court and is the final interpreter of the Constitution. The most powerful of the nine Supreme Court justices is the chief justice.

Federal judges are appointed by the president and must be approved by the Senate. They then serve for life, although they are subject to impeachment. Appointing federal judges is one of the most important acts of a president, as these judges shape the nature of the judiciary and may influence the interpretation of the law for many years after the president who appointed them leaves office. The president takes the leading role in choosing nominees for the Supreme Court. In recent years, the nominations of justices such as Robert Bork and Clarence Thomas, whose views were perceived to be controversial, received intense examination. Justices with moderate views, however, have received bipartisan support.

The judiciary interprets statutes and constitutional provisions. The power of federal courts to decide whether the acts of the executive and legislative branches of government are constitutional is called judicial review. Although not mentioned in the Constitution, judicial review was established in the 1803 case, *Marbury* v. *Madison*. Restrictions on the courts include the power of Congress to impeach and remove judges, Congress's ability to change the jurisdiction of federal courts, and Congress's ability to pass legislation or constitutional amendments to change Supreme Court decisions. Other constraints on the courts include the appointment power of the president and public opinion. Some judges exercise great self-control when exercising their judicial power while others favor a policy of judicial activism and are more likely to declare actions of other branches unconstitutional.

The history of the Supreme Court consists of three periods. From 1800 to 1865, the Court was concerned primarily with issues of federalism. From 1865 to 1938, the Court dealt with issues of a growing industrial society, including child labor laws and other laws related to the concerns of workers. From 1938 to the present, the Court has focused largely on issues of civil rights and civil liberties. These decisions have been of great importance, as they clarify the extent of the freedom of citizens from illegal and arbitrary governmental actions.

## KEY TERMS

administrative law
adversary system
advisory opinions
appellate jurisdiction
briefs
civil law
common law
concurring opinions
constitutional courts
constitutional law
criminal law
defendant
dissenting opinions
equity
felonies
impeachment
injunction
judicial activism

judicial review
judicial self-restraint
jurisdiction
law
legislative courts
"living Constitution"
majority opinion
misdemeanors
original jurisdiction
plaintiff
senatorial courtesy
*stare decisis*
statutory law
textualism
treaties
writ of *certiorari*
writ of *mandamus*

# PRACTICE EXERCISES

## FILL IN THE BLANKS

1. The principle of applying existing precedents to legal cases involving similar facts is known as _____ _____.

2. A _____ law is based on formal declaration by a legislature.

3. Regulations issued by administrative agencies of the federal, state, or local governments are known collectively as _____ law.

4. Because of our federal form of government, the United States has a _____ court system which refers to the fact that we have a federal court system as well as fifty state court systems.

5. Granted either by a constitution or by legislative statute, the right of a court to hear a particular type of case is called _____.

6. Today, most states select their judges through a(n) _____ process, rather than by direct election.

7. Article III, Section I of the U.S. Constitution gives the power to establish inferior courts (those below the Supreme Court) to _____.

8. When a trial court's decision is appealed, lawyers for the opposing party file a _____, or a written argument stating why the lower court's decision should not be overturned.

9. An opinion written by a judge to record his disagreement with the majority decision and to express his reasons for voting against it is called a _____ opinion.

10. An order directing a lower court to send the record of a case to the Supreme Court for review is called a writ of _____.

## MULTIPLE CHOICE

11. Law based on a set of generally accepted rules that were created by judges in the course of rendering decisions is called
    a. equity.
    b. statutory law.
    c. constitutional law.
    d. common law.

12. Law that deals with acts that endanger the public welfare is
    a. civil law.
    b. common law.
    c. criminal law.
    d. constitutional law.

13. A(n) _____ system is a legal system based on the idea that, when there are disputes between parties, the truth will emerge from the clash of opposing interests.
    a. adversary
    b. opposing
    c. constitutional
    d. common law

14. The body of law which deals primarily with disputes between private individuals or corporations and defines the rights of the parties in the dispute is
    a. administrative law.
    b. equity.
    c. criminal law.
    d. civil law.

15. Courts created by Congress that hear matters concerning specific policy areas are called
    a. civil courts.
    b. tribunals.
    c. statutory courts.
    d. legislative courts.

16. A court that reviews the decisions of lower courts to determine whether they applied the correct rule of law has
    a. original jurisdiction.
    b. statutory authority.
    c. appellate jurisdiction.
    d. concurrent jurisdiction.

17. The Supreme Court is a(n)
    a. federal legislative court.
    b. trial court.
    c. constitutional court.
    d. statutory court.

18. Cases involving disputes between two states are heard by the Supreme Court and most often involve
    a. immigration issues.
    b. taxation issues.
    c. environmental issues.
    d. boundary issues.

19. A vast majority of civil and criminal cases are brought in
    a. state courts.
    b. federal courts.
    c. appellate courts.
    d. juvenile courts.

20. From 1800 until the end of the Civil War in 1865, the Supreme Court was concerned primarily with issues related to
    a. civil rights.
    b. federalism.
    c. slavery.
    d. social and economic reform legislation.

21. The Supreme Court asserted the doctrine of judicial review in the case of
    a. *Muskrat* v. *United States*.
    b. *Marbury* v. *Madison*.
    c. *Brown* v. *Board of Education of Topeka*.
    d. *Buckley* v. *Valeo*.

22. A court order to a public official to perform a legally required act is called a
    a. warrant.
    b. writ of *mandamus*.
    c. writ of *certiorari*.
    d. restraining order.

23. A judge who defers to elective branches of government and does not make policy by judicial decision is acting consistent with the philosophy of
    a. original intent.
    b. judicial self-restraint.
    c. judicial activism.
    d. judicial decree.

24. Since the late 1930s, the U.S. Supreme Court has been concerned primarily with issues related to
    a. federalism.
    b. regulation of business and industry.
    c. civil liberties and civil rights.
    d. economic and social reform legislation.

25. Judicial review refers to the federal courts' ability to
    a. hear appeals.
    b. determine the constitutionality of legislative and executive actions.
    c. oversee the legislative operations of the states.
    d. review and approve military plans.

## TRUE OR FALSE

26. In general, felonies are less serious violations of law than misdemeanors.
T F

27. The twentieth century has seen a shift toward more statutory law and less common law.
T F

28. The primary question in *Marbury* v. *Madison* was whether the Supreme Court had the authority to issue a writ of *mandamus*.
T F

29. In the history of the U.S. judicial system, no federal judge has ever been both impeached and convicted and removed from office.
T F

30. The most common means for a case to reach the U.S. Supreme Court is by a writ of *certiorari*.
T F

## DISCUSSION, ESSAY

31. Identify and describe the five basic types of law.

32. Explain why the U.S. legal system is referred to as an adversary system.

33. Discuss the role of the judiciary in U.S. politics. Does the Supreme Court have too much or too little power? Explain your answer.

34. Distinguish between judicial self-restraint and judicial activism. Are there ideological aspects associated with each? Explain.

35. How have the types of issues facing the Supreme Court changed over time?

36. Explain why George W. Bush encountered difficulty with his judicial nominations during the 2001-2005 period. What could he have done differently to avoid this conflict?

# CHAPTER 11
# CIVIL LIBERTIES

## CHAPTER OVERVIEW

Chapter 11 reviews individual rights, or civil liberties, guaranteed by the Constitution and the due process clause of the Fourteenth Amendment. The chapter describes how the Supreme Court has extended most of the provisions of the Bill of Rights to the states and expanded the scope of civil liberties through interpretation of the Bill of Rights.

The chapter identifies the various provisions of the Bill of Rights, including freedom of religion, freedom of speech, press, assembly, and petition, and the rights of the criminally accused, and discusses how the Supreme Court has interpreted these provisions in particular cases. The chapter outlines key issues that the Supreme Court has considered in cases involving the Bill of Rights and how the understanding of civil rights has developed and changed over time.

First to be discussed are the free exercise clause, which prohibits the government from restricting religious expression, and the establishment clause, which limits government involvement with religion. Next, the chapter focuses on freedom of expression, the concept of prior restraint, and the lack of constitutional protection for speech that is obscene, defamatory, or highly inflammatory.

The chapter also reviews the constitutional rights of criminal defendants, including protection from warrantless searches, freedom from self-incrimination and double jeopardy, the prohibition of cruel and unusual punishment, and the guarantee of a court-appointed lawyer for indigent defendants.

Also included is a section discussing the detention and treatment of enemy soldiers captured during times of war under the Geneva Convention and how those terms do not apply to civilian terrorists.

The chapter concludes by discussing how the personal philosophies of Supreme Court justices influence the decisions made by the Supreme Court and identifying changing interpretations of civil liberties by the courts.


## LEARNING OBJECTIVES

1.  Describe the relationship between the Bill of Rights and the Constitution.
2.  Explain how the Bill of Rights applies to the states, paying particular attention to the process of incorporation.
3.  Explain the guarantees provided under the First Amendment and outline their major exceptions.
4.  Assess the impact of the *Miranda* case on the protections afforded to those charged with a crime.
5.  Define the exclusionary rule of evidence and explain its importance in criminal law for civil liberties.
6.  Define the prior restraint doctrine and explain its importance.

# CHAPTER OUTLINE

I.    Introduction/Applying the Bill of Rights to the states
    A. 1833 Supreme Court ruling (*Barron* v. *Baltimore*)
    B. Selective incorporation
    C. Civil liberties and the due process clause

II.   Freedom of religion (*Reynolds* v. *United States*, 1878)
    A. The free exercise clause and the issue of "compelling interest"
    B. The establishment clause
        1. Aid to parochial/religious schools (*Lemon* v. *Kurtzman*, 1971)
        2. School prayer (*Engel* v. *Vitale*, 1962)
        3. Religious displays on public property (secular purpose or not?)

III.  Freedom of speech, press, assembly, and petition
    A. Censorship: The rule against prior restraint (*The Pentagon Papers* case)
    B. Sedition: Advocacy of illegal acts
        1. *Dennis* v. *United States* (1951) — test of Smith Act
        2. *Brandenburg* v. *Ohio* (showing of "imminent danger" necessary)
    C. Protecting public order: The First Amendment in public places
        1. *Chicago* v. *Morales* (1999)
    D. Protecting public morals: Obscenity
        1. *Roth* v. *United States* (1957)
        2. *Miller* v. *California* (1973)
    E. Libel and slander (*New York Times* v. *Sullivan*, 1964)
    F. The First Amendment and campaign spending
        1. *Buckley* v. *Valeo* (1976)
        2. 2002 Campaign Finance Reform Act faces constitutional test
    G. The right of association
    H. Commercial speech
    I.  Symbolic speech
    J.  Free press and a fair trial

IV.   The rights of the criminally accused
    A. Constitutional provisions limiting the powers of government in relation to the criminally accused
    B. Search and seizure
    C. The exclusionary rule (*Mapp* v. *Ohio*,1961)
    D. Electronic and other forms of surveillance (*Katz* v. *U.S.*, 1967)
    E. Freedom from self-incrimination
    F. Indictment by a grand jury
    G. Double jeopardy
    H. The right to counsel (*Gideon* v. *Wainwright*, 1963)
    I.  The right to an impartial jury
    J.  Confessions (*Miranda* v. *Arizona*, 1966)
    K. "Cruel and unusual punishment" and the death penalty
        1. *Atkins* v. *Virginia* (2002) —mentally retarded could not be executed
        2. Death penalty on federal level (Timothy McVeigh)

V.    Detainees and the war on terrorism
    A. Geneva Convention and the treatment of enemy soldiers during times of war
    B. Treatment of civilian detainees at Guantanamo Bay
    C. Military Commission Act of 2006

# CHAPTER SUMMARY

The rights outlined in the Bill of Rights were designed to protect citizens against abuses of power by the government. They were derived from the knowledge of history and colonial experiences with British rule. The individual rights that are guaranteed by the Constitution, especially in the Bill of Rights and the due process clause of the Fourteenth Amendment, are referred to as civil liberties.

In 1833, the Supreme Court held that the Bill of Rights applied only to the national government and not to the state governments. Under the due process clause of the Fourteenth Amendment, however, nearly all of the limitations identified in the Bill of Rights have been extended to the states. This process is referred to as selective incorporation. The only major provision of the Bill of Rights that has been not applied to the states is the Fifth Amendment requirement of indictment by a grand jury.

The First Amendment states: "Congress shall make no law respecting an establishment of religion or prohibiting the free exercise thereof." This statement identifies two limits on government with respect to religion. The second clause of this statement, the free exercise clause, prohibits the government from limiting the right to hold and express religious beliefs. In its interpretation of the free exercise clause, the Supreme Court has stated that although religious beliefs are protected by the First Amendment, certain religious practices may be prohibited. In the 1878 case of *Reynolds* v. *the United States*, the court held that even though polygamy was sanctioned by the Mormon religion at the time, it was in violation of a federal law prohibiting bigamy. The Court found that religious freedom includes the right to any personal religious belief but not the right to commit illegal acts.

The second limit on government with respect to religion is identified in the establishment clause, the first part of the First Amendment's statement regarding freedom of religion. The establishment clause has been the center of greater controversy than the free exercise clause, with debate centering on three major concerns: aid to religious or parochial schools, prayers and Bible reading in schools, and religious displays on public property. The Supreme Court has found most forms of public aid to religious schools to be unconstitutional. Conservative justices on the current Supreme Court, however, have been critical of earlier cases involving the establishment clause, and future Court decisions in this area are likely to be influenced by this change in Supreme Court views.

In the 1962 case of *Engel* v. *Vitale*, the Supreme Court held that school prayer was in violation of the establishment clause. Similarly, the Court has found Bible reading in public schools to be in violation of the Constitution. The establishment clause has also been at issue in a number of Supreme Court cases involving the display of religious symbols on public property. The facts of these cases have differed greatly, and the Supreme Court has made decisions on a case-by-case basis.

In addition to religious freedom, the First Amendment also guarantees freedom of speech, press, and assembly. As with religious freedom, however, these rights are not unlimited. In the case of what the Supreme Court has identified as "fighting words," for example, words said directly to a person that are likely to cause a breach of peace are subject to restriction by the government.

With respect to freedom of the press, the Supreme Court has prohibited all forms of prior restraint of speech, arguing that this would deny the public total access to ideas and information. The no prior restraint doctrine was established in constitutional law in the case of *Near* v. *Minnesota*, which declared a Minnesota state law that allowed police officers to prevent the publication of newspapers containing "malicious, scandalous or defamatory" statements to be unconstitutional.

In cases of sedition, where speech or writing advocates or incites acts against the government, the Supreme Court has determined that there are limits on such speech. The Supreme Court set forth the current standard for determining the constitutionality of prosecutions for sedition in the case of *Brandenburg* v. *Ohio*. In *Brandenburg*, the Court found that speech that can be shown to impose an imminent danger may be limited. Speech that calls for revolutionary change or action against the government that does not pose an imminent danger, however, is protected under the *Brandenburg* decision.

The First Amendment guarantee of freedom of assembly may conflict with the maintenance of public order, and the Supreme Court has supported limits on the freedom of assembly in public places dedicated to a particular purpose and in limited circumstances that do not discriminate against particular individuals or groups. A demonstration that might interfere with the normal operation of school activities, for example, could be prohibited in the area of the school.

Another area of First Amendment concern is obscenity. Since the 1950s, the Supreme Court has attempted to set standards for assessing whether a movie, book, or other published material is obscene. Defining obscenity has proven difficult, however, and the legal standards in this area are not firmly established.

In the area of defamation, including libel and slander, the Supreme Court has found that the First Amendment protects neither libel nor slander. Public officials, however, have a more difficult time suing for defamation, as the Supreme Court has said that public figures have voluntarily surrendered their privacy in a way that private persons have not.

Other issues of First Amendment concern include restrictions on campaign spending as potential violations of the right to free speech, the extent of the right of association, and the protection of commercial speech and symbolic speech. There are also situations where First Amendment rights may clash with other provisions of the Bill of Rights. In highly publicized trials, for example, the First Amendment guarantee of freedom of the press can clash with the Sixth Amendment right of an individual to receive a fair trial. In a widely publicized case, a defendant may argue that it is difficult to find an impartial jury that has not been prejudiced by media coverage of the case.

The Constitution limits the powers of government in relation to people accused of crimes in a number of ways. The prohibition of *ex post facto* laws and bills of attainder are included in the original text of the Constitution. Most of the rights of accused criminals, however, are included in the Bill of Rights.

The Fourth Amendment requires that routine police searches and seizures be conducted with a search warrant. Under the exclusionary rule, evidence obtained as a result of an illegal search and seizure cannot be used in a case against an alleged criminal. There has been significant criticism of the exclusionary rule, however, and the Supreme Court has allowed several exceptions to the rule. Electronic surveillance, which allows surveillance and gathering of evidence without entry into a home or business, is another area of controversy under the Fourth Amendment.

Other constitutional guarantees to those accused of crimes are included in the Fifth, Sixth, and Eighth Amendments. The Fifth Amendment to the Constitution guarantees freedom from self-incrimination, the right to indictment by a grand jury, and protection against double jeopardy. The Sixth Amendment guarantees that in criminal cases, accused individuals will be provided lawyers. The Sixth Amendment also provides the right to an impartial jury. The Eighth Amendment prohibits "cruel and unusual punishment."

Since the 1970s, the prohibition on cruel and unusual punishment has been used to challenge the constitutionality of the death penalty. The Supreme Court, however, has upheld the constitutionality of the death penalty, provided that certain standards are met. The limitations on the death penalty include a restriction to those convicted of murder, separation of the determination of guilt or innocence from sentencing, and lack of discrimination in the application of the death penalty. In addition, in June 2002, the Supreme Court invalidated the laws of eighteen states that allowed the execution of retarded persons and, in 2005, the Court held that the execution of persons under the age of 18 at the time the crime was committed violated the Fifth Amendment's prohibition against "cruel and unusual punishment."

Enemy soldiers captured during times of war are protected under international law, most notably the Geneva Conventions. These protections are not extended to civilian soldiers who are suspected of terrorism. Suspected civilian terrorists are subject to indefinite detention, trial before military tribunals instead of civilian juries, looser standards of evidence, and closed proceedings, among other practices. The constitutionality of these treatments is under Supreme Court review; in particular, an act of Congress, the Military Commission Act of 2006, is to be reviewed in the fall of 2007. This act pertains to the treatment of the Iraqi and Afghani terrorist suspects who are being detained by the United States at Guantanamo Bay.

The Supreme Court's interpretation of the guarantees of the Bill of Rights has developed and changed over time. Despite differences in the scope of civil liberties depending on Supreme Court decisions, the extent of individual liberty in the United States is expansive. Political and religious freedom is widespread, and accused criminals are broadly protected from the power of government.

## KEY TERMS

| | |
|---|---|
| bill of information | grand jury |
| civil liberties | indictment |
| commercial speech | libel |
| compelling interest | prior restraint |
| defamation | sedition |
| double jeopardy | selective incorporation |
| due process clause | self-incrimination |
| establishment clause | slander |
| exclusionary rule of evidence | *voir dire* |
| free exercise clause | |

## PRACTICE EXERCISES

### FILL IN THE BLANKS

1.   The First Amendment guarantees of religious freedom include the free exercise clause and the _____ clause.

2.   The three-part test developed by the Supreme Court in 1971 to determine whether a law violates the establishment clause is called the _____ test.

3.   The Supreme Court has upheld government's right to punish the use of "obscene," "libelous," and "insulting," or _____ words because they are likely to cause a breach of the peace.

4. Speech or writing that advocates rebellion against the government is known as _____.

5. In *Miller* v. *California*, the Court decided that the tests for obscenity could be determined by applying _____ standards.

6. According to the Supreme Court, the Constitution offers private individuals greater protections against defamatory statements than _____ _____.

7. If a grand jury believes that the government has enough evidence to warrant a criminal trial of a person accused of a crime, it returns a(n) _____.

8. The _____ _____ established an international standard regarding the manner in which prisoners taken during times of war must be treated.

9. New laws that impose a penalty for committing an act that was not considered criminal when it was committed are unconstitutional. These laws are called _____ _____ _____ laws.

10. The act that legalized the use of _____ surveillance for police investigations, but required officers to first obtain a warrant, is the Omnibus Crime Control and Safe Streets Act of 1968.

MULTIPLE CHOICE

11. Individual rights that are guaranteed in the Bill of Rights are
   a. civil rights.
   b. civil liberties.
   c. natural rights.
   d. natural liberties.

12. The due process clause is part of the
   a. First Amendment.
   b. Tenth Amendment.
   c. Fourteenth Amendment.
   d. statutes passed by federal and state legislatures.

13. The process of applying the limitations of the Bill of Rights to the states is called
   a. selective incorporation.
   b. exclusionary.
   c. *voir dire*.
   d. establishment.

14. Aid to parochial schools has caused controversy because some believe that it violates the First Amendment's _____.
   a. establishment clause
   b. free exercise clause
   c. freedom of assembly clause
   d. compelling interest clause

15. The first major case to deal with freedom of religion was
    a. *Miller* v. *California*.
    b. *Engel* v. *Vitale*.
    c. *Torasco* v. *Walkins*.
    d. *Reynolds* v. *United States*.

16. A provision of the Child Pornography Prevention Act (1996) that made it a crime to create and distribute "virtual" child pornography was declared unconstitutional due to which case?
    a. *Miller* v. *California*.
    b. *Ashcroft* v. *Free Speech Coalition*.
    c. *Torasco* v. *Walkins*.
    d. *Reynolds* v. *United States*.

17. The case of *Near* v. *Minnesota* established the
    a. no prior restraint doctrine.
    b. exclusionary rule of evidence.
    c. *Lemon* test.
    d. *Miranda* rules.

18. The actual malice rule of the *Sullivan* case applies to
    a. obscenity.
    b. commercial speech.
    c. freedom of association.
    d. defamation.

19. The *Pentagon Papers* dispute of 1971 was an important Supreme Court case involving
    a. freedom of religion.
    b. symbolic speech.
    c. prior restraint.
    d. libel.

20. The exclusionary rule of evidence is intended to
    a. deter illegal searches and seizures by the police.
    b. provide for *voir dire*.
    c. protect against self-incrimination.
    d. protect against double jeopardy.

21. A person who does not take the stand in his or her defense in a criminal trial cannot be presumed guilty due to the Fifth Amendment protection against
    a. self-incrimination.
    b. double jeopardy.
    c. illegal search and seizure.
    d. cruel and unusual punishment.

22. The 1963 case, *Gideon* v. *Wainright,* established
   a. the right to *voir dire.*
   b. the extension of the right to an attorney to include all state felony trials.
   c. the extension of the right to a bill of information to include all state felony trials.
   d. protection against double jeopardy.

23. If a grand jury believes that the government has enough evidence to bring a person accused of a crime to trial, it issues a(n)
   a. writ of *habeas corpus.*
   b. plea bargain.
   c. indictment.
   d. sentence.

24. The Supreme Court formally recognized the right of association as a derivative of the freedoms protected by the First Amendment in the landmark case,
   a. *NAACP* v. *Alabama.*
   b. *Buckley* v. *Valeo.*
   c. *Sheppard* v. *Maxwell.*
   d. *United States* v. *Eichman.*

25. The Geneva Convention establishes which of the following?
   a. that prisoners taken during times of war be treated humanely by the nations who hold them
   b. that prisoners taken during times of war should be released to neutral nation-states
   c. that prisoners taken during times of war must be released within 60 days of capture
   d. that wartime prisoners may be harshly interrogated if a warrant is first obtained

TRUE OR FALSE

26. Civil liberties are concerned with protection against discrimination.
   T F

27. Displaying religious symbols on public property has consistently been declared unconstitutional by the Supreme Court.
   T F

28. According to the Bush administration, the terms of the Geneva Convention apply to the detainees at Guantanamo Bay.
   T F

29. Commercial speech may be regulated if it is false or misleading.
   T F

30. Since the 1970s, the Supreme Court has significantly broadened the interpretation of the rights of the criminally accused.
   T F

DISCUSSION, ESSAY

31.    Distinguish between civil liberties and civil rights.

32.    Explain the relationship of the Bill of Rights to the states.

33.    Discuss how the rapid growth of the Internet raises difficult issues related to freedom of speech. Include examples of recent court cases.

34.    Identify and discuss the Supreme Court's position with respect to electronic surveillance.

35.    Identify the constitutional rights of the criminally accused. Include a discussion regarding "cruel and unusual punishment" in relation to state death penalty laws.


## ABC NEWS/PRENTICE HALL VIDEO LIBRARY: AMERICAN GOVERNMENT

### LIFE OR DEATH DECISION, PART 2
**Originally Aired: 3/22/05**
**Program: *Nightline***
**Running Time: 16:25**

The Terri Schiavo case is the ultimate "on the one hand, on the other hand" debate. Each aspect of this debate—legal, medical, political, even the moral and ethical—has a deep rift of opinions. And all sides were watching the 11th Circuit Court of Appeals in Atlanta for the next step in this case.

A federal judge denied a request for an emergency order to restore Terri Schiavo's feeding tube. The judge took the position that the lawyers representing her parents were unlikely to succeed in a resulting federal trial. Her parents immediately appealed the case to the 11th Circuit. If the Schindlers, Shiavo's parents, lose there, it will almost certainly be taken quickly to the U.S. Supreme Court, which has already declined to hear the case three times. But in the meantime, Terri Schiavo is in her fourth day without nutrition. Doctors say she could live another week or more without food or water. And so the debate rages on, with all sides staking out firm positions. In the medical debate, there are those that point to the evidence that her brain function is irreversibly damaged. But on the other hand, there is the loving care that her parents have shown for their profoundly disabled daughter.

The intervention of Congress turned this into a major political battle. On the one hand, there are right-to-life advocates who see this as another test of the sanctity of life. On the other hand, there are those who are offended at Congress for inserting itself into a family tragedy. And finally, there are the ethical issues that are at the heart of so many of these factors—the medical, the legal, and the political. If you believe it is wrong, simply wrong, to remove a feeding tube in order to expedite death, how can you ever accept any of the other arguments? And on the other side, if you believe Michael Schiavo is holding strong for his wife's stated intentions, how can you ever accept any of the other arguments?

On this program, George Stephanopoulos discusses all of these matters—medical, legal, political, and ethical—with a panel of guests.

## Critical Thinking Questions

1. Given that the Terry Schiavo case had spent years in state court, on what grounds was the case sent to federal court?

2. The experts in "Life or Death Decision, Part 2" differentiate between the right to die and the right to refuse unwanted medical intervention. Describe the differences between these two concepts.

3. Those that supported keeping Terri Schiavo alive often referred to her right to due process under the Fourteenth Amendment. To what do you think they were referring? Would procedural due process apply to this case? Would substantive due process apply to this case?


## CRIME & PUNISHMENT
**Originally Aired: 12/1/04**
**Program: Nightline**
**Running Time: 13:57**

Voting to have a man or woman put to death has to be one of the hardest decisions facing any American juror. How do we ever know for sure if the person convicted of the crime actually committed it? One death row prisoner in Texas served 17 years for a crime he didn't commit, and Ernest Willis's case was built entirely on circumstantial evidence. At one point, he was days away from being executed, but now he is a free man.

Ernest Willis, who on four different dates was scheduled for execution, learned in October 2004 that he would be exonerated and released from prison. After years of appeals, litigation, and the drive of a young lawyer in a large law firm, Willis was completely exonerated of the murder charges that put him on death row. ABC correspondent Mike von Fremd was at the prison when he was released after 17 years. They sat down for a conversation about how he ended up on death row, his feelings on facing execution, his surprising release, and what it was like to finally meet the woman he had married while he was in prison. Texas puts more prisoners to death than any other state.

## Critical Thinking Questions

1. One reason appeals courts often overturn a death sentence is due to the incompetence of the defendant's attorney. As an example of this, describe the problems with Ernest Willis's attorney in "Crime & Punishment."

2. In "Crime & Punishment," Ori White, the Pecos County, Texas, district attorney, says prosecutors often feel that "the ends justify the means." What do you think he meant by this?

3. More than two-thirds of all death sentences are overturned on appeal. On what grounds are they overturned?

**ILLEGAL IMMIGRANT WORKERS**
**Originally Aired: 12/14/04**
**Program: *Nightline***
**Running Time: 15:22**

When Bernard Kerik, President Bush's first choice to run the Department of Homeland Security, withdrew his nomination because of a nanny who was an undocumented worker that he hired and failed to pay taxes on, it was a story that probably sounded familiar. Cabinet nominees have been tripped up on this issue before in both the Clinton and Bush administrations. So the question is why does this keep happening?

One of the reasons it keeps happening is that it is pretty easy to get by hiring undocumented workers. It seems that the only way to get tripped up is if you undergo a background check for an important government post. You would be hard pressed to find any aspect of the nation's economy where undocumented workers are not making a contribution. It could be in the service industry or the construction business. You will eat something today that has been brought to you as a result of the labor of illegal immigrants working here. A conservative estimate is that at least 50 percent of agricultural laborers are undocumented workers. So is this a result of American employers being cheap or is it a result of the efficiency of market forces? Many employers say it is not easy to find Americans willing to do a lot of the low-paying, menial, and tedious tasks that immigrants are willing to do. Labor advocates say that illegal immigrants depress the wage market so Americans are shut out of these jobs. Everyone can find statistics to back their argument.

So what is the solution? When the president announced a proposal earlier this year to grant legal status to millions of undocumented workers in the United Stated, it wasn't greeted with unanimous enthusiasm. "Out of common sense and fairness, our laws should allow willing workers to enter our country and fill jobs that Americans are not filling," the president said. He wasn't calling for amnesty but a temporary guest worker program. But will that satisfy both sides? Michel Martin examines the arguments advanced on something that has always been a hot-button issue. We also speak with Senator John McCain of Arizona. His state has addressed the illegal immigration issue by voting for a sweeping proposition that bans all government services to illegal immigrants. He says that this is an issue that the nation has to wake up to and start dealing with as a high priority.

### *Critical Thinking Questions*

1. Why aren't immigration laws more strictly enforced?

2. Explain the "geographic" component to immigration law enforcement.

3. The inability to bar illegal aliens from entering the country is not a question of power. Rather, the problems are political and practical. Briefly explain what this means.

## CHURCH & STATE, AND PLEDGE OF ALLEGIANCE
**Originally Aired: 7/8/02**
**Program: *Nightline***
**Running Time: 14:44**

Where does religion fit into American politics? In light of the furor over the decision by a federal appeals court on the 'Pledge of Allegiance,' what about 'In God We Trust'? Does this country treat religion differently than other countries? *Nightline* looks at the connection between church and state.

### *Critical Thinking Questions*
1. Why are voters so interested in a candidate's religion, according to "Church & State, and Pledge of Allegiance"?

2. Under what circumstances was the phrase "under God" made part of the Pledge of Allegiance?

3. Justice Sandra Day O'Conner's "endorsement test" has been the basis of several Supreme Court decisions. What is it and how might it apply to the Pledge of Allegiance?


## VOICES OF DISSENT
**Originally Aired: 11/2/01**
**Program: *Nightline***
**Running Time: 12:10**

Disagreement is an essential component of one of America's most cherished freedoms: the right to free speech. On this program, *Nightline* makes room for voices representing opinions that are likely to be less popular or less mainstream than what is normally heard in the media.

### *Critical Thinking Questions*
1. In "Voices of Dissent," author Arundhati Roy says, "Operation Enduring Freedom is ostensibly being fought to uphold the American way of life. It'll probably end up undermining it entirely." What does she mean by this?

2. In "Voices of Dissent," cartoonist Aaron McGroder says that "in the six days after the bombing, America became the most intensely stupid place on the planet." Why does McGroder believe this to be true?

3. While Americans overwhelmingly support the principle of free speech, many do not support the freedom to say things with which they disagree. Why might it be even more important to protect free speech in times of crisis than in normal times?

**MUSLIMS IN AMERICA**
**Originally Aired: 5/4/95**
**Program:** *Nightline*
**Running Time: 13:41**

*Nightline* looks at one of the fastest growing groups in America: Muslims. Members of the oldest Muslim community in Cedar Rapids, Iowa, speak to Ted Koppel about their beliefs and customs.

### *Critical Thinking Questions*

1. Differentiate between Arabs and Muslims.

2. The video, "Muslims in America," gives several possible explanations why, even before 9/11, Americans were quick to blame Muslims for every terrorist act. Briefly discuss two explanations.

3. If the equal protection clause applies only to the actions of governments, how may we limit the discriminatory actions of private individuals?

# CHAPTER 12
# CIVIL RIGHTS

## CHAPTER OVERVIEW

Chapter 12 explores the history of civil rights in the United States. The chapter distinguishes civil rights from civil liberties and defines civil rights as involving issues of equality and freedom from discrimination. The chapter identifies the constitutional foundations of civil rights as the equal protection clause of the Fourteenth Amendment; the Thirteenth, Fifteenth, Nineteenth, and Twenty-fourth Amendments; the due process clause of the Fifth Amendment; and the power of Congress to enact civil rights legislation.

The chapter first discusses the history of discrimination against nonwhites in the United States, including Native Americans, blacks, Hispanics, and Asians. The chapter identifies the Supreme Court case of *Brown* v. *Board of Education* and the Civil Rights Act of 1964 as marking important changes in the legal treatment of blacks and other nonwhite minorities in the United States.

The chapter next reviews the development of the women's rights movement in the United States, including the fight for women's suffrage and the adoption of the Nineteenth Amendment, the failure of the Equal Rights Amendment, issues involving equality in employment, and arguments concerning abortion and the constitutional rights of women.

Chapter 12 then discusses the civil rights of the disabled and the Americans with Disabilities Act of 1990, affirmative action, and the right to vote. The chapter concludes with a brief review of progress in guaranteeing civil rights to all U.S. citizens.

## LEARNING OBJECTIVES

1.  Outline the major provisions and requirements of the Civil Rights Act of 1964.
2.  Outline the major provisions and requirements of the Voting Rights Act of 1965.
3.  Discuss the main arguments for and against affirmative action and assess the program's effectiveness.
4.  Explain how the Supreme Court decides the constitutionality of laws based on gender.
5.  Assess the evolution of the struggle for women's rights during the past few decades and examine the major factors that have caused this evolution.
6.  Outline the major provisions of the Americans with Disabilities Act.

## CHAPTER OUTLINE

I.  The rights of African Americans
    A. Historic struggle for rights
       1. The Missouri Compromise
       2. The *Dred Scott* decision
       3. The Emancipation Proclamation
       4. Civil War amendments
       5. Movement away from racial equality
          a. Civil Rights Cases of 1883
          b. *Plessy* v. *Ferguson* (1896)
          c. Jim Crow laws

B. School desegregation
    1. *Sweatt* v. *Painter*
    2. *Brown* v. *Board of Education of Topeka*
    3. Segregation in the North
        a. *De facto* segregation
        b. *De jure* segregation
C. Civil Rights Act of 1964
    1. Title II: Equality in public places
    2. Title VII: Equality in employment
    3. Title IX: Equality in education

II.    Women's rights
A. History
    1. Seneca Falls convention
    2. Nineteenth Amendment
    3. Failure of the Equal Rights Amendment
B. Equality in employment
C. Equality in education
D. The Constitution and women's rights
    1. Abortion-related cases
        a. *Roe* v. *Wade*
        b. *Webster* v. *Reproductive Health Services*
        c. *Planned Parenthood* v. *Casey*
        d. Partial birth abortion
    2. Sex-based discrimination cases
        a. *Reed* v. *Reed*
        b. *United States* v. *Virginia*

III.    Affirmative action
A. Definition
B. Quota-based affirmative-action plans
    1. Arguments for quota systems
    2. Arguments against quota systems
C. Supreme Court rulings on the constitutionality of affirmative-action programs
    1. *Regents of the University of California* v. *Bakke*
    2. *City of Richmond* v. *J.A. Croson Company*
    3. The 2002-2003 University of Michigan cases: *Grutter v. Bollinger* and *Gratz* v. *Bollinger*

IV.    The civil rights of the disabled
A. Rehabilitation Act of 1973
B. Education for All Handicapped Children Act of 1974
C. Americans with Disabilities Act of 1990
D. Supreme Court restricted term "disability" in 2002

V.    The right to vote
A. The Fifteenth Amendment
B. Barriers to African American voting
    1. The grandfather clause
    2. The white primary
    3. Poll taxes
    4. Literacy tests
C. The Voting Rights Act of 1965

# CHAPTER SUMMARY

Civil rights are rights associated with equality and freedom from discrimination. The constitutional foundations for the protection of civil rights include the equal protection clause of the Fourteenth Amendment and the due process clause of the Fifth Amendment.

The struggle for civil rights for blacks in the United States has a long history. Questions concerning the civil rights of women, Hispanics, the disabled, and other minority groups have developed more recently. The history of civil rights in the U.S. involves the fight for expansion of civil rights to include blacks and other nonwhite minorities, women, and the disabled.

Racial discrimination in America dates back to the seventeenth-century treatment of Native Americans by European settlers. Native American lands were taken, and Native Americans were forced onto reservations. Blacks were brought to the American colonies as slaves. Slaves were brought to both the North and the South, but the plantation economy in the South became dependent on slaves, whereas the northern economy did not. As the differences between the North and South became greater, the issue of slavery came to the forefront of politics in the United States.

In 1857, the Supreme Court attempted to resolve the issue of slavery by ruling in the *Dred Scott* decision that slaves were not citizens, but this only served to exacerbate conflict on the issue. Slavery was ended with the Civil War and the Emancipation Proclamation of 1863. In 1865, the Thirteenth Amendment to the U.S. Constitution permanently outlawed slavery. The Fourteenth and Fifteenth Amendments were passed in an attempt to give blacks the full rights of citizens.

Despite the post-Civil War constitutional amendments and civil rights laws designed to enforce them, blacks were systematically denied the rights of white citizens. In the 1896 case, *Plessy* v. *Ferguson,* the Supreme Court established the separate-but-equal doctrine. This gave constitutional protection to so-called Jim Crow laws, which segregated blacks and whites in most public and private institutions and facilities in the southern states, regardless of whether the separate facilities were indeed equal. In both the North and South, blacks and ethnic minority populations faced discrimination in housing, employment, and other areas.

In response to discrimination, groups such as the NAACP were formed to work for the civil rights of minority group members. During the 1930s, the NAACP adopted a legal strategy designed to challenge the separate-but-equal doctrine in the federal courts. The group focused its efforts on the education system and, after more than 20 years, achieved the goal of overturning the separate-but-equal doctrine.

In the 1954 case, *Brown* v. *Board of Education of Topeka,* the Supreme Court concluded that separate educational institutions for blacks and whites were "inherently unequal." A year later, the Court ordered that local public school districts must end segregation "with all deliberate speed." It was not until the Civil Rights Act of 1964 and federal financial aid for public education in 1965, however, that desegregation actually began in earnest. In the 1960s and 1970s, the Supreme Court authorized a variety of means to achieve integration, including court-ordered busing of children from their home neighborhoods to schools in other areas of their school system. In 1991, the Supreme Court found that busing should be ended when illegal segregation was no longer present. In some areas, segregated schools are the consequence of what is called *de facto* segregation: segregation that occurs as a result of housing patterns and the decisions made by private citizens. Moreover, some black educators question whether black children benefit from racially mixed schools. Thus, the issue of school desegregation has not been resolved entirely.

Another important goal of civil rights advocates, such as the NAACP, was equal access to public facilities such as restaurants, buses, theaters, and hospitals. Beginning with the Montgomery bus boycott in 1955, large-scale demonstrations, protests, and sit-ins finally led to the passage of the Civil Rights Act of 1964. Title II of this law forbids discrimination in public facilities because of race, color, religion, or national origin. Other portions of the Civil Rights Act of 1964 forbid discrimination in employment and discrimination in education.

The women's rights movement in the United States is traced back to an 1848 convention held in Seneca Falls, New York, which adopted resolutions calling for equal rights for women in business, property, contracts, and marriage. In 1920, the Nineteenth Amendment gave women the right to vote. The Equal Rights Amendment (ERA), which would have guaranteed equal rights for men and women, passed in Congress in 1972, but the amendment fell short of the 38 states required for ratification by three votes.

Despite the failure of the ERA, the women's movement has achieved a number of legislative and judicial victories. Many state and local governments have passed legislation to forbid discrimination against women, and federal laws such as the Civil Rights Act of 1964 have been applied to protect the rights of women. The courts have recognized sexual harassment as a modern form of employment discrimination, and in 1973, the Supreme Court's *Roe* v. *Wade* decision recognized a constitutional right to an abortion. The *Roe* decision, however, has been extremely controversial. In recent years, the Supreme Court has allowed states greater freedom to place restrictions on access to abortion.

Another issue in the area of civil rights for minority groups and women is affirmative action. Affirmative action refers to a variety of policies and programs designed to reverse the effects of past discrimination and advance the position of minority group members; these policies and programs have been very controversial. The Supreme Court has issued a number of rulings on affirmative action programs, and Court justices appointed by Presidents Reagan and Bush have not been supportive of government-sponsored affirmative action programs.

In the area of civil rights for the disabled, the Americans with Disabilities Act of 1990 bars discrimination against the disabled in employment, transportation, public accommodations, and telecommunications. This act, which affects an estimated 45 million Americans, is comparable in scope to the Civil Rights Act of 1964. In 2002, the Supreme Court somewhat restricted the meaning of the term "disability" by "requiring not only proof that the individual suffered from substantial limitations to work-related activities but also to those that are central to daily life."

A final area of importance in the history of civil rights is the right to vote. The Fifteenth Amendment, adopted in 1870, decreed that the right to vote should not be denied on the basis of race. Despite this, the efforts of African American citizens to vote were frustrated by devices such as the grandfather clause, poll taxes, and literacy tests. It was not until the Voting Rights Act of 1965 that black Americans were provided protection by federal law and the violation of their right to vote was ended. Since then, blacks have made significant advances in voter turnout and election to public office.

# KEY TERMS

affirmative action
civil rights
class action
*de facto* segregation
*de jure* segregation
grandfather clause
Jim Crow laws
literacy test

poll taxes
reasonableness test
separate-but-equal doctrine
skeptical scrutiny
strict scrutiny
substantiality test
white primary

# PRACTICE EXERCISES

## FILL IN THE BLANKS

1.      The _____ Amendment to the U.S. Constitution permanently outlawed slavery.

2.      In the case *Brown* v. *Board of Education of Topeka*, the Supreme Court found that segregation in the area of public _____ is inherently unequal and unconstitutional.

3.      The NAACP was founded by _____ and other prominent civil rights leaders to protect and advance the interests of African Americans.

4.      Segregation that results primarily from housing patterns and decisions made by private citizens is called _____ segregation.

5.      Lawsuits filed by a person or persons on behalf of representatives of a group of similar persons are called _____ suits.

6.      Women received the right to vote in 1920 with the passage of the _____ Amendment to the U.S. Constitution.

7.      In the Supreme Court case *Planned Parenthood* v. *Casey,* the Court recognized an _____ _____ law adopted by Pennsylvania that required, among other things, women under the age of 18 to obtain written consent from their parent or guardian.

8.      Programs created by government and private organizations that are designed to provide greater opportunities for women, African Americans, and other minority groups who have been victims of past discrimination are called _____ _____ programs.

9.      The _____ _____ _____ _____ of 1990 bars discrimination against the disabled in employment, transportation, public accommodations, and telecommunications.

10.     The 1982 amendment to the Voting Rights Act of 1965 allows discriminatory voting practices to be evaluated by the _____ of the practice rather than having to prove that it was the intention of the government to discriminate.

MULTIPLE CHOICE

11. Civil rights are different from civil liberties in that civil rights
    a. involve the right not to be discriminated against because of some characteristic, such as national origin or disability.
    b. involve the right to free speech.
    c. are not guaranteed under the Constitution.
    d. are identified in the Bill of Rights.

12. The equal protection clause, which provides a basis for the protection of civil rights, is part of the
    a. First Amendment.
    b. Second Amendment.
    c. Fourteenth Amendment.
    d. Fifteenth Amendment.

13. In the Civil Rights Cases of 1883, the Supreme Court took a narrow view of the Fourteenth Amendment and found that
    a. the separate-but-equal doctrine was unconstitutional.
    b. Jim Crow laws were unconstitutional.
    c. slaves were not citizens.
    d. the Fourteenth Amendment did not bar private acts of discrimination.

14. Jim Crow laws
    a. forbade racial segregation in public and private institutions.
    b. permitted racial segregation in public and private institutions.
    c. forbade discrimination on the basis of sex.
    d. permitted discrimination on the basis of sex.

15. Since the *Roe* v. *Wade* decision in 1973, the Supreme Court
    a. has overturned its decision to allow abortion as a constitutional right.
    b. has allowed states to restrict aspects of abortion as long as the restrictions do not place an "undue burden" on women seeking abortions.
    c. has forced states to comply with complete and free access to abortions.
    d. has ordered Congress to pass legislation to make abortions available at no cost to the woman.

16. In which case was the separate-but-equal doctrine rejected by the Supreme Court as the governing principle in cases involving public education?
    a. *Sweatt* v. *Painter*
    b. *Plessy* v. *Ferguson*
    c. *Brown* v. *Board of Education of Topeka*
    d. *McCulloch* v. *Maryland*

17. The aim of the 1955 boycott of the bus company in Montgomery, Alabama, was to
    a. get the bus company to allow women to be hired as bus drivers.
    b. end the busing of children to achieve integration of the schools.
    c. end racial segregation on the buses and allow equal access for blacks.
    d. end the threat of a class-action suit against the bus company.

18. The law that forbids discrimination in public places because of race, color, religion, or national origin is the
a. Civil Rights Act of 1875.
b. Public Facilities Act of 1954.
c. Equal Access Act of 1960.
d. Civil Rights Act of 1964.

19. The government agency that has the power to investigate complaints of job discrimination and bring lawsuits against private employers is the
a. Federal Trade Commission (FTC).
b. Employment Discrimination Commission (EDC).
c. Equal Employment Opportunity Commission (EEOC).
d. Equal Rights Commission (ERC).

20. Although there are none on the federal level, nineteen states protect homosexuals with
a. affirmative action policies.
b. same-sex marriage laws.
c. antidiscrimination and hate crime laws.
d. sexual orientation education policies.

21. The Supreme Court defines a hostile work environment as one in which
a. any job is denied to a person based on gender.
b. discrimination, ridicule, or intimidation is severe or pervasive.
c. men and women cannot work together because of gender-related issues.
d. any person feels physically threatened.

22. In the cases of *Webster* v. *Reproductive Health Services* and *Planned Parenthood* v. *Casey*, the Supreme Court indicated willingness to
a. apply the strict scrutiny test to laws involving limits on abortion.
b. give states greater freedom to control access to abortion.
c. give states less freedom to control access to abortion.
d. allow states to prohibit abortion.

23. In *United States* v. *Virginia,* the Supreme Court held that the Virginia Military Institute's history of admitting only males
a. was an unconstitutional violation of the equal protection clause of the Constitution.
b. was not an unconstitutional violation of the equal protection clause of the Constitution because a similar military program at a Virginia women's college accepted females.
c. was not unconstitutional because it met the test of strict scrutiny.
d. was not unconstitutional because it met the reasonableness test.

24. In 2007, the Supreme Court upheld Congress's 2003 ban on _____ _____ abortion, stating that it did not place "an undue burden" on a woman's right to obtain an abortion.
a. first trimester
b. late term
c. gender specific
d. partial birth

25. Following the Fifteenth Amendment's ratification, many southern states enacted the grandfather clause which
   a. allowed only the elderly to vote.
   b. allowed only those previously registered with a major party to vote.
   c. allowed only those who weren't freed slaves to vote.
   d. allowed only those who had voted before 1866 or were descended from one who voted before 1866 to vote.

TRUE OR FALSE

26. In 2007, the Supreme Court ruled that it is unconstitutional to use race as a basis for assigning students to particular public schools.
   T F

27. In the Civil Rights Cases of 1883, the Supreme Court ruled that Congress could pass legislation to end discrimination by both government and private individuals.
   T F

28. Desegregation of schools in the South did not begin in an important way until schools in the South faced the loss of federal financial aid for education.
   T F

29. Due to protection by the Fourteenth Amendment, the Supreme Court overturned a Texas sodomy law that made it a crime for two persons of the same sex to engage in certain sexual acts.
   T F

30. The successful passage of the Equal Rights Amendment was an important victory for the women's rights movement in the United States.
   T F

DISCUSSION, ESSAY

31. Trace the history of civil rights for black Americans using key Supreme Court decisions and constitutional amendments as your basis.

32. Identify civil rights groups formed to promote the rights of racial and ethnic minorities and women, and discuss the extent to which the techniques used by these groups have been successful.

33. Describe the origins and history of the women's rights movement in the United States.

34. Identify and describe important legislation regarding discrimination against the disabled, and compare this legislation to legislation passed on behalf of racial and ethnic minorities.

35. The Civil Rights Acts of 1964 addressed discrimination in America. Discuss the various titles, or sections, that pertain to equality in public places, employment, and education.

# CHAPTER 13
## PUBLIC POLICY—WHAT GOVERNMENT DOES

## CHAPTER OVERVIEW

Chapter 13 focuses on public policy and the policy-making process. The chapter describes public policy as arising in response to problems in society and identifies the stages in policy making and the context and structure of policy making. The chapter examines three specific areas of domestic policy: fiscal policy, monetary policy, and social welfare.

The chapter begins by defining public policy and reviewing various theories of how public policy is developed. The chapter then discusses the various ways that political scientists characterize public policies, reviews the stages of policy making, and briefly describes the environment and organization of policy making. The chapter continues with a discussion of economic policy and explains the difference between fiscal policy and monetary policy.

The chapter then turns to social-welfare policy, which touches on fundamental questions about the role of government in protecting the well-being of individuals. The chapter identifies how welfare policies in the United States differ from most European democracies and describes several approaches the U.S. government has taken in the realm of social welfare policies. The chapter concludes with a discussion of welfare reform legislation passed in 1996 and how the economic turndown that began in 2000 challenged the new welfare system. Finally, the chapter discusses Congress's attempts to encourage states to emphasize work for those people on their welfare rolls.

## LEARNING OBJECTIVES

1. List and explain the major policy areas on the current congressional agenda.
2. Analyze the different theoretical approaches to policy and explain how they differ from each other.
3. Explain and discuss the differences between fiscal and monetary policy.
4. Explain the three major areas of foreign policy. Discuss each one and how they differ from each other.
5. Compare and contrast federal and state welfare policies.

## CHAPTER OUTLINE

I. What is public policy?
   A. A definition of public policy
   B. Who makes public policy?
      1. Group theory
      2. Elite theory
      3. Corporatism
      4. Subgovernments

C. Types of public policy
    1. Regulatory, distributive, or redistributive
    2. Material or symbolic
    3. Substantive or procedural
    4. Liberal or conservative
    5. Domestic or foreign

II.    The policy-making process
    A. Stages of the process
        1. Issue identification and agenda setting
        2. Policy formulation and adoption
        3. Policy implementation
        4. Policy evaluation
    B. The context of policy making
        1. History of past policies
        2. Environmental factors
        3. Ideological conflict
        4. The budgetary process
    C. The structure of policy making
        1. Rational-choice model
        2. Incrementalist model

III.    Economic policy
    A. Fiscal policy (raising/lowering of tax rates, controlling government spending)
    B. Monetary policy (control inflation through the money supply)
        1. Milton Friedman
        2. Federal Reserve Board
    C. Other economic policy tools

IV.    Social-welfare policy
    A. Welfare policies in the United States and European democracies
    B. Categories of welfare policies
        1. Policies that benefit the poor
        2. General assistance programs
    C. Approaches to providing social welfare
        1. Preventive approach
        2. Alleviative approach
        3. Punitive approach
        4. Curative approach
        5. Incomes approach
    D. Welfare policy in the United States
        1. New Deal programs
        2. Great Society programs
        3. Personal Responsibility and Work Opportunity Act of 1996
        4. Economic turndown of 2000 and its impact

## CHAPTER SUMMARY

        Public policy is purposeful, goal-oriented action that is designed to deal with problems that arise in society. Public policy generally produces one or more of the following: reconciliation of conflicting claims over scarce resources, creation of incentives for collective action, limits on morally unacceptable action, protection of the rights and activities of individuals and groups, or provision of direct benefits to individuals. Different models have been used to explain the public policy process and who controls and benefits from it, including group theory, elite theory, corporatism, and the notion of subgovernments.

Public policies can be characterized in different ways, including regulatory, distributive, or redistributive; material or symbolic; substantive or procedural; liberal or conservative; and domestic or foreign.

Political scientists have developed a framework for studying the policy-making process that identifies several sequential stages: issue identification and agenda setting, policy formulation, policy adoption, policy implementation, and policy evaluation. Although the policy-making process may be divided into distinct stages, it is important to recognize that the process is a complex series of ongoing events rather than a set of separate steps.

The process of policy making is influenced by a number of major factors, including the history of policies in a particular policy domain; cultural, social, and ideological concerns; and the budgetary process. Political scientists disagree about the nature of policy making, and two distinct models have been developed to explain how policy decisions are actually made: the rational choice and incrementalist theories.

Since the end of World War II in 1945, the policy agenda in the United States has centered on economic and foreign policies. Two major views of economic policy have guided the nation since the 1930s. The first is Keynesian economics, which stresses fiscal policy. Fiscal policy refers to the taxing and spending powers of the government, and Keynesian economists advocate the use of taxation and government spending to influence economic productivity and the business cycle, and to limit inflation and unemployment. The second view of economic policy is monetarism, which emphasizes control of the nation's money supply. Monetarists emphasize the importance of controlling inflation by controlling the money supply of a nation. The Federal Reserve Board plays a prominent role in monetary policy based on its power to raise and lower interest rates.

In addition to fiscal and monetary policies, the government uses other economic instruments to influence the national economy. These include the reduction of tariffs and the removal of other barriers to international trade, and the reduction of governmental restrictions on business and industry through deregulation. The federal budget deficit, which had reached over $290 billion in 1992, steadily decreased from 1993 to 1997, and by the turn of the century, the national government produced the first budget surplus since the late 1960s. The emergence of a new information economy, the policies of President Clinton and the Republican-controlled Congress, and the policies of Federal Reserve Chairman Alan Greenspan are credited with producing a sustained period of economic growth, low inflation, low unemployment, and the budget surplus. However, the budgetary surplus disappeared during the Bush administration, which caused a serious economic turndown. The September 11 terrorist attacks accelerated the economy's problems.

Social-welfare policy refers to the provision of basic social necessities such as education, health care, and housing. The welfare policies of the United States differ in a number of ways from the welfare policies of European democracies. Welfare programs in the United States began later than welfare programs in Europe, and the United States generally provides fewer welfare services than European democracies.

Social-welfare policies are classified into two broad categories: policies that benefit the poor and general assistance programs that benefit individuals regardless of level of income. General assistance programs receive greater public support than policies that benefit the poor. General assistance programs include Social Security, Medicare, and unemployment insurance. Welfare programs for the poor became a major focus of the national policy agenda in the 1980s and 1990s. In 1996, Congress passed the Personal Responsibility and Work Opportunity Act, which made major changes in the nation's welfare programs for the poor. There have been positive results from these changes in welfare, but critics remain concerned about the long-term consequences of reform. In 2006, Congress reenacted TANF, a cash assistance program that requires job participation for those receiving welfare.

## KEY TERMS

| | |
|---|---|
| agenda | pluralism |
| corporatism | procedural policies |
| distributive policy | process evaluation |
| elite theory | public policy |
| fiscal policy | redistributive policy |
| group theory | regulatory policy |
| impact evaluation | subgovernments |
| implementation | substantive policies |
| issue | symbolic policies |
| material policies | welfare |
| monetary policy | |

## PRACTICE EXERCISES

### FILL IN THE BLANKS

1.   The model that views public policy as the result of competition among groups is called group theory or _____.

2.   Iron triangles refer to the relationships among government agencies, congressional committees, and _____ _____.

3.   _____ policies have no material impact and no tangible advantages or disadvantages.

4.   _____ policies are concerned with how something will be done and who will perform the task.

5.   The consequences of a policy are examined to assess the effectiveness of the policy in the policy _____ stage of policy making.

6.   The process of building support for a proposed policy is known as policy _____.

7.   _____ economic theory emphasizes the importance of controlling inflation by controlling the nation's money supply.

8.   Based on its power to raise and lower interest rates, the _____ _____ _____ plays a central role in the nation's monetary policy.

9.    In _____ _____, a large number of programs are available to help people in times of distress, such as when they lose jobs, become sick, or are otherwise unable to support themselves.

10.   An _____ approach to providing social welfare requires individuals to work while they receive government assistance.


MULTIPLE CHOICE

11.   Which model of public policy making is sometimes referred to as "iron triangles"?
      a. group theory
      b. elite theory
      c. subgovernments
      d. corporatism

12.   Which model of public policy making assumes that interests not only seek to influence policy but also seek to become part of the policy-making and implementation process?
      a. group theory
      b. elite theory
      c. subgovernments
      d. corporatism

13.   Policies that reallocate resources among groups in society are classified as
      a. material.
      b. redistributive.
      c. conservative.
      d. procedural.

14.   When social welfare policies seek to remedy the conditions that cause poverty, they are _____ in nature.
      a. punitive
      b. curative
      c. conservative
      d. flawed

15.   Policies that seek government action to achieve social or economic gain are classified as
      a. symbolic.
      b. liberal.
      c. conservative.
      d. procedural.

16.   Policies that favor private, nongovernmental solutions to problems are classified as
      a. regulatory.
      b. liberal.
      c. conservative.
      d. distributive.

17. The stage of the policy-making process that involves developing proposals for dealing with an issue is the
   a. issue identification stage.
   b. policy implementation stage.
   c. policy formulation stage.
   d. agenda setting stage.

18. The program that has often been referred to as "the third rail" of U.S. politics because elected officials fear defeat in their next election if they propose changes to the program is
   a. unemployment insurance.
   b. Medicaid.
   c. Aid for Families with Dependent Children (AFDC).
   d. Social Security.

19. An agreement between two nations to *not* impose taxes on one another's goods is an example of which type of policy?
   a. domestic policy
   b. foreign policy
   c. regulatory policy
   d. procedural policy

20. The aspect of policy evaluation that examines the extent to which a policy is implemented according to stated guidelines is called
   a. process evaluation.
   b. implementation evaluation.
   c. impact evaluation.
   d. guideline evaluation.

21. The model that views policy making as a process in which issues and problems are identified, various alternative policy solutions are considered, and the policy solution that is chosen is the solution most appropriate for achieving the desired policy outcome is called
   a. incrementalism.
   b. corporatism.
   c. procedural.
   d. rational choice.

22. The economist most closely associated with monetary policy is
   a. Milton Friedman.
   b. John Maynard Keynes.
   c. Harold Lasswell.
   d. John Locke.

23. When the Federal Reserve Board has believed in recent years that the economy was growing too strongly and inflation was a threat, they have acted to
   a. decrease interest rates.
   b. raise interest rates.
   c. decrease taxes.
   d. raise taxes.

24. The United States differs from European democracies such as Great Britain and Germany in that
    a. social welfare programs such as Social Security were adopted earlier in the United States.
    b. social welfare programs in the United States generally provide more services and benefits.
    c. social welfare programs in the United States generally provide fewer services and benefits.
    d. social welfare programs in the United States require a larger percentage of the nation's gross domestic product (GDP).

25. The approach to social welfare that is often used when the goal of a policy is to give the poor greater control over the institutions that affect their communities is called the
    a. incomes approach.
    b. curative approach.
    c. alleviative approach.
    d. punitive approach.

TRUE OR FALSE

26. One of the biggest problems with government-operated pension plans today is that the elderly population is growing while the number of workers contributing to the pension program is declining.
    T  F

27. Although public policy may involve governmental factors primarily, private organizations and groups may also play a significant role in public policy.
    T  F

28. Impact evaluation is concerned with measuring change against an ideal standard, whereas process evaluation deals with the actual nature of any changes that have occurred.
    T  F

29. The United States, like most European democracies, provides universal health coverage.
    T  F

30. Welfare policies fall into one broad category: policies that benefit the poor.
    T  F

DISCUSSION, ESSAY

31. Discuss the four models that help to explain who controls and benefits from the policy-making process.

32. Research a problem that became the basis for a policy program. Using this policy as an example, identify the stages of the policy-making process.

33. Describe the various components that make up the context of policy making.

34.    Identify the different approaches to social welfare that the U.S. government has used, and discuss the advantages and disadvantages of these distinct approaches.

35.    Explain the main features of fiscal policy and monetary policy, including the administrations that have attempted to use them and the outcome of those attempts.


## ABC NEWS/PRENTICE HALL VIDEO LIBRARY: AMERICAN GOVERNMENT

**ON THE EDGE**
**Originally Aired: 4/15/04**
**Program: *Nightline***
**Running Time: 16:16**

When we say "poor" or "poverty-stricken Americans," what image comes to mind? The homeless man sleeping on the grate? The unemployed person standing in line at the unemployment or welfare office? What about someone who has a full-time job making $9 an hour? That sounds like a decent wage, right? Well, that actually comes out to just above $18,000 a year, and for a family with one adult and three children, that means poverty. We've decided to launch a new, occasional series that looks at the working poor: the millions of Americans who live on the edge of poverty.

The genesis of tonight's show was a new book by former *New York Times* reporter and Pulitzer Prize-winner, David Shipler. *The Working Poor* takes a comprehensive look at the lives of people set to plunge into the abyss of financial ruin if just one payment isn't met, if their car breaks down, or if they call in sick to work. Such seemingly minor events can have catastrophic effects on this segment of the population, and Mr. Shipler has documented many of their lives, weaving economic analysis into the story of what these people face trying to survive from day to day. Ted Koppel sat down with Mr. Shipler for an extensive interview on his findings.

### Critical Thinking Questions

1. How does author David Shipler define "working poor"?

2. How does the video's title, *On the Edge*, apply to the working poor?

3. The underlying problem of the working poor seems to be their vulnerability in every area of life. Explain how the working poor are vulnerable in ways not experienced by other economic groups.

4. Author David Shipler disagrees with the concept of a "culture of poverty." Instead, he speaks of an "ecological system of interactions." What does he mean?

5. What is the difference between an entitlement and a means-tested entitlement?

# CHAPTER 14
# FOREIGN POLICY


## CHAPTER OVERVIEW

Chapter 14 focuses on U.S. foreign policy. The chapter begins by distinguishing and describing two broad theories of international relations: realism and liberalism. These theories aim to explain the behavior of nations based on the sources of competition, conflict, and cooperation among nations. The chapter identifies how realism and liberalism are reflected in U.S. foreign policy and provides historical examples of each. Next, the chapter describes the domestic context of U.S. foreign policy, including governmental and societal sources that influence U.S. foreign policy.

The chapter concludes with a brief consideration of how U.S. foreign policy may develop in the future, especially in the light of the September 11 attacks and the U.S. war against international terrorism.


## LEARNING OBJECTIVES

1.    Compare and contrast realism and liberalism.
2.    Define and discuss the internal and external sources of foreign policy.
3.    Define and discuss the concept of *balance of power*.
4.    Explain the historical and contemporary importance of the Monroe Doctrine.
5.    Define and discuss the concept of *collective security*.
6.    Define and discuss *multilateralism*.


## CHAPTER OUTLINE

I.    Competing theories of international relations
      A. Realism
         1. Anarchic international system
         2. Balance of power
         3. Realism and American foreign policy
            a. The Monroe Doctrine
            b. The emergence of the United States as a global power
            c. World Wars I and II
            d. The Cold War
      B. Liberalism
         1. President Wilson and World War I
         2. Contemporary liberalism
         3. Selective engagement
         4. Liberalism and realism as enduring perspectives
II.   The Post-Cold War period
      A. The United States as the sole global superpower
      B. First and second-tier nations
      C. Multilateralism
      D. Promotion of democracy and market capitalism abroad

III. The rise of international terrorism
  A. Terrorism as "premeditated, politically motivated violence"
    1. Hits noncombatant groups
    2. Used by subnational groups
    3. May involve hostage taking, bombings, assassinations
    4. On September 11, Al Qaeda terrorists hit World Trade Center/Pentagon
  B. United States removed Taliban regime in Afghanistan
  C. United States removed Saddam Hussein regime in Iraq
  D. The preemption doctrine
    1. Critics view doctrine as encouraging U.S. aggression
IV. American foreign policy: The domestic context
  A. Governmental sources
    1. The president
    2. The executive branch
    3. Congress
  B. Societal sources
    1. Interest groups
    2. The media

## CHAPTER SUMMARY

To understand a nation's foreign policy, it is necessary to consider a number of different influences. These influences may be classified as external (or systemic) or internal (or domestic). Systemic factors are elements of the international environment and include military, economic, and political characteristics of other nations. Domestic factors are elements of the political, economic, and social forces within a nation. Smaller and weaker nations are more susceptible to influence by systemic factors, whereas more powerful nations, such as the United States, are better able to influence the international environment according to their own preferences.

Success in foreign policy depends upon the ability of policymakers to identify sensible and appropriate foreign policy goals. These goals are based on both fundamental national interests that endure over time and interests that change over time. There are two broad theories of international relations that have been used to explain the interests that have guided U.S. foreign policy over the last two centuries. Realism, the first of these theories, has been the dominant approach to U.S. foreign policy. Despite the dominance of realism, liberalism, the second theory, has coexisted as an explanation for United States' action in the international arena.

Realists maintain that cooperation among nations is limited by competition among nations in an anarchic international system without a supreme political authority. Nations with stable, legitimate political systems enjoy a hierarchy of political power and authority, and political institutions have both the means and perceived legitimacy to make rules and enforce them. Conversely, in the international arena, nations are free to define and pursue their interests and there is no hierarchical authority to enforce standards of conduct.

In the realist view, the international environment is a competitive arena dominated by fear and insecurity where nations seek to maximize power. The distribution of resources and capabilities among nations are a major influence on foreign policy, and the most powerful nations have strong incentives to compete for power in the military, economic, and political arenas. Over the long run, aggressive nations or allied nations that seek to dominate the international system encourage the development of countervailing forces that oppose them, and a balance of power or equilibrium may result from these countervailing forces. Over the course of U.S. history, the nation's foreign policy has tended to promote either a stable balance of power or dominance by the United States.

U.S. citizens have often disagreed about the proper role of the nation in the world, but there has been a broad, durable consensus on the central interests of the nation. The United States has always sought dominance in the Western Hemisphere; this is reflected in the Monroe Doctrine of 1823, which insisted that no non-American nation could interfere in the affairs of the Western Hemisphere. The European nations of Britain, France, Germany, and Russia have historically been viewed as the greatest threat to U.S. dominance in the Western Hemisphere, and the United States has consistently sought to prevent the emergence of a power among these nations that could threaten U.S. dominance.

During the 1800s, the United States remained largely isolated from power politics in Europe and primarily behaved in a unilateral fashion, without the cooperation or approval of other nations. At the same time, the United States became more involved in the Western Hemisphere. By 1900, the United States was in a position to defend its hegemonic position as the dominant nation in the Western Hemisphere from attempts by European powers to challenge the U.S. position. The United States also adopted mercantilist policies, policies based on the idea that wealth and power go together, which involved expanding U.S. involvement in international trade.

When Theodore Roosevelt became president in 1901, he adopted a more interventionist role in the international arena. This is expressed in the Roosevelt Corollary to the Monroe Doctrine, which justified U.S. intervention in the internal politics of Latin American nations. The United States occupied Cuba and became involved in the domestic affairs of other nations, and the nation emerged as a global influence in international affairs.

United States intervention in World War I helped to maintain the balance of power in Europe, and following World War II, the U.S. emerged as the dominant power on any continent. The United States helped to rebuild the economies of Western Europe and Japan following the war and helped to negotiate treaties that created the North Atlantic Treaty Organization (NATO) and other regional security alliances. Europe became divided between two hostile alliances: NATO, including the United States and like-minded democracies; and the Warsaw Pact, an alliance controlled by the Soviet Union, including East Germany, Hungary, Czechoslovakia, Poland, and other nations. During the Cold War that followed, full-scale war between NATO and the Warsaw Pact was prevented by the fear on both sides of nuclear world war. There were, however, wars in Korea and Vietnam between U.S. forces and forces supported by the Soviet Union.

The experience of the United States in Vietnam, in particular, led to reduced willingness to send U.S. troops abroad and to a less militaristic policy of détente with the Soviet Union. The Cold War ended with the break-up of the Soviet Union and the Warsaw Pact, and the United States emerged as the sole global superpower and maintained a leadership position in NATO. It is possible that the European Union, Japan, China, or a combination of Japan and China could become a threat to U.S. security in the future, but this remains to be seen.

It is possible to interpret much of the history of U.S. foreign policy from the realist perspective of the struggle for power in an anarchic international environment. Liberalism, the second theory of international relations, however, has been an alternative explanation for U.S. foreign policy from the founding of the nation to the present. Liberalism in this meaning emphasizes the importance of individual, political, and economic liberty as central values influencing the interests of a nation. In the view of utopian liberals, including President Woodrow Wilson, the realist pursuit of national interest alone was seen as both immoral and ineffective at preventing wars among great powers. Wilson was committed to the idea of collective security and the creation of an international organization designed to maintain world order and cooperation among nations. Peace would be ensured by the commitment of nations belonging to this international organization to act in a unified and overwhelming response against any act of aggression against a member nation. The principles of liberalism were reflected in the League of Nations, developed at the end of World War I. The U.S. Senate, however, defeated President Wilson's attempt to have the United States join the League of Nations.

Following World War II, the United Nations was founded as a means to maintain world peace, based on principles of liberalism similar to those behind the League of Nations. Realists, however, contend that the United Nations illustrates the failure of liberal principles in foreign policy and the value of the realist view of anarchy in the international arena. The United States, for example, has refused to pay monetary dues to the United Nations. Lacking the authority and power of a national government such as the U.S. government, the UN is unable to compel the United States to pay its dues.

Given examples such as this, contemporary liberals acknowledge the insights of a realist view of foreign policy. Liberals contend, however, that anarchy in the international arena does not prevent the development of cooperation, civility, or order among nations. Liberals point to increasing economic interdependence and the importance of democratic institutions for promoting compromise and fostering cooperation among nations. Liberals, in short, have a more optimistic view of the potential for avoiding conflict and war in the international arena.

The endurance of realism and liberalism as perspectives for understanding U.S. foreign policy reflects the competing objectives that have shaped U.S. foreign policy over time. At the same time that the United States has wanted to ensure national security, it has wanted to serve as a model for other nations. The pursuit of both of these objectives, however, has sometimes led to contradictory policies. During the Cold War, for example, the United States wanted to promote democracy and free markets throughout the world. In Cold War conflict with the Soviet Union, however, the United States supported nondemocratic and even repressive leaders in nations that allied with the U.S. against communism. In the post-Cold War world, the United States no longer faces the threat of communist expansion.

The post-Cold War foreign policy of the United States was transformed by the events of September 11, 2001. The September 11 attacks by terrorists upon American soil (World Trade Center towers and the Pentagon, resulting in over 3,000 deaths) ushered in a new war by the United States against international terrorism. Terrorism is defined as "premeditated, politically motivated violence against noncombatant targets by subnational groups." Accordingly, the United States sent military forces to oust the Taliban government in Afghanistan, a regime that supported Osama bin Laden's Al Qaeda terrorist network. President Bush also directed his attention to other states engaged in the sponsorship of terrorism and/or the production of weapons of mass destruction (nuclear, biological, chemical). Three such states—Iraq, Iran, and North Korea—were labeled by Bush as an "axis of evil." After Afghanistan, the Bush administration singled out Saddam Hussein's Iraq as the second "regime change" target, since Saddam had ignored repeated United Nations resolutions to destroy its weapons of mass destruction while frustrating UN inspectors inside of Iraq. Despite misgivings by Germany,

France, and Russia, the United States assembled a coalition to remove Saddam from power. In March-April of 2003, U.S. and British forces destroyed Saddam's army and occupied the country. The post-war objective was to create a democratic Iraq. Insurgence began in response to the occupation and has continued through 2007. The military actions taken against Afghanistan and Iraq were justified by President Bush according to the doctrine of "preemption," meaning that the United States would not wait for terrorists to strike its soil first and then retaliate. It would actively seek out staging areas for terrorism and/or states that supported those terrorists, and, if necessary, use its military force (alone, if there was no other way) to eliminate those threats. In short, the United States would do all it could to prevent nuclear, biological, or chemical attacks. Critics of the preemption doctrine argued that it justified the United States' aggressive actions against nations and could lead to an exhaustion of American resources through endless, multiple conflicts overseas.

The liberal view of foreign policy places greater emphasis on the influence of domestic factors on foreign policy, and domestic factors are of particular importance in a hegemonic nation such as the United States. The nation is less susceptible to international pressures and threats, and many domestic actors and interests seek to influence the nation's foreign policy. Within the government, the president, the executive branch, and Congress each try to assert dominance in decisions about foreign policy. Because the Constitution divides the powers of foreign policy between the executive and Congress, a struggle for influence over foreign policy ensues.

Over the course of U.S. history, the president and the executive branch have gained power in the realm of foreign policy. Congress, however, remains an important player in the conduct of foreign affairs. President Clinton, for example, unsuccessfully attempted to gain passage of legislation involving the payment of U.S. dues to the United Nations and other international aid. In November 1999, the Senate refused to pass the Comprehensive Test Ban Treaty, a major defeat for the Clinton administration's foreign policy objectives.

There are also nongovernmental influences on U.S. foreign policy. A wide array of interest groups, ranging from business and labor interests to ethnic groups seeking to influence a particular aspect of U.S. foreign policy, compete to shape policy in ways that often conflict. In addition, the media influence international policy in a number of ways. The stories that are covered in the media influence the foreign policy agenda and the issues that are seen as important in the international arena, and technological advances in media have compressed the process of making foreign policy decisions into a shorter time frame.

The factors that influence U.S. foreign policy are diverse and complex. The end of the Cold War has left the United States as the world's sole superpower. Other nations, however, have interests that may conflict with U.S. interests, and the global distribution of power changes over time. Within the nation, there are competing interests, as well. It seems unlikely that the United States will withdraw from its leadership position in the world, but conflicting interests and values, both internationally and domestically, provide for alternative potential outcomes.

# KEY TERMS

anarchy
balance of power
collective security
containment
détente
hegemon
isolationism
liberalism
mercantilism
Monroe Doctrine

multilateralism
policy influentials
preemption
realism
*realpolitik*
Roosevelt Corollary
selective engagement
terrorism
unilateralism

# PRACTICE EXERCISES

## FILL IN THE BLANKS

1. The theory of international relations that views the behavior of nations as guided by the absence of a supreme political authority in the international arena is _____.

2. _____ means to act without the approval or cooperation of other nations.

3. The 1823 statement that sought to safeguard the United States from European interference in the Western Hemisphere was the _____ _____.

4. President Theodore Roosevelt embraced a harsh and unsentimental position, _____, as his guiding philosophy in foreign policy.

5. The dominant state or world power is called a(n) _____.

6. _____ policies are based on the assumption that the wealth and power of a nation are linked and that a nation should pursue policies such as subsidizing domestic industries to increase national wealth.

7. The "axis of evil" nations referred to Iraq, _____, and _____ _____.

8. Mikhail Gorbachev was the first Soviet leader to allow the free expression of _____ _____ that might threaten the legitimacy of Soviet rule.

9. The period of more favorable relations with the Soviet Union that followed the Vietnam War was characterized by a policy known as _____.

10. U.S. relations with China demonstrate the idea that _____ interdependence will prevent nations with fundamental differences from fighting.

MULTIPLE CHOICE

11. A core concept of realism is
    a. corporatism.
    b. détente.
    c. anarchy.
    d. mercantilism.

12. In the _____ _____, the United States insisted that no non-American nation may interfere in the affairs of the Western Hemisphere.
    a. Panama Treaty
    b. Monroe Doctrine
    c. Aggression Resolution
    d. PATRIOT Act

13. During the 1800s, U.S. foreign policy was characterized largely by
    a. unilateralism.
    b. multilateralism.
    c. containment.
    d. collective security.

14. The harsh and unsentimental pursuit of national interests is called
    a. realpolitik.
    b. anarchy.
    c. containment.
    d. isolationism.

15. Woodrow Wilson encouraged _____ _____, secured by multinational membership in an international organization dedicated to maintaining order and cooperation.
    a. collective security
    b. community relations
    c. conflict resolution
    d. selective engagement

16. The statement that justified U.S. intervention in the domestic politics of Latin American nations was the
    a. Monroe Doctrine.
    b. farewell address of William McKinley.
    c. Roosevelt Corollary to the Monroe Doctrine.
    d. Truman Doctrine.

17. Contemporary liberalism recognizes many of the realist perspectives but asserts that international _____ does/do not bar common interests, civility, or order.
    a. alliances
    b. engagement
    c. anarchy
    d. cooperation

18. The alliance formed between the United States and Western European nations after the end of World War II is the
   a. League of Nations.
   b. United Nations.
   c. Organization of the United States and Europe.
   d. North Atlantic Treaty Organization.

19. The war that lasted thirty years and spanned six presidential administrations, culminating in defeat, was
   a. World War I.
   b. World War II.
   c. the Korean War.
   d. the Vietnam War.

20. _____ _____ derives from the works of thinkers such as Emmanuel Kant, John Locke, Adam Smith, and Thomas Jefferson. It translates into foreign policy by providing an emphasis on individual political and economic liberty.
   a. Classical conservatism
   b. Classical liberalism
   c. Economic determinism
   d. Classical realism

21. The notion of _____ _____ involves the use of U.S. military power to prevent major threats to American security, especially by helping to prevent wars from breaking out among the great powers of the world.
   a. preemptive action
   b. peaceful containment
   c. organized anarchy
   d. selective engagement

22. The end of the Cold War elicited much optimism that the _____ _____ _____ was imminent, leading to the triumph of Western liberal economic and democratic values.
   a. end of mercantilism
   b. end of history
   c. end of anarchy
   d. end of tyranny

23. The United States' efforts to move former communist nations into market economies have
   a. been very successful.
   b. caused many other communist nations to follow suit.
   c. led to the end of communism in the world.
   d. had mixed results.

24. Which of the following policy options, if adopted, would most likely lead the United States to ignore humanitarian disasters and conflicts that do not threaten U.S. security interests?
a. multilateralism
b. unilateralism
c. selective engagement
d. neo-liberal institutionalism

25. Terrorist activities are motivated by
a. economic sanctions.
b. different political ideologies.
c. competition for weapons of mass destruction.
d. containment policies.

TRUE OR FALSE

26. President Bush has used the policy of preemption to justify actions taken against international terrorism.
T  F

27. The years between World War I and World War II were characterized largely by isolationism in U.S. foreign policy.
T  F

28. U.S. foreign policy is strongly susceptible to influence by forces in the international arena.
T  F

29. Prior to the attacks of September 11, there had been no terrorist strikes upon United States soil.
T  F

30. The president is the central governmental source of U.S. foreign policy.
T  F

DISCUSSION, ESSAY

31. Identify and describe the key differences between realism and liberalism in international relations.

32. Explain the position that the Supreme Court has played in foreign affairs. Explain the cases that involve the Court in foreign policy and why the Court decided to involve itself.

33. Identify the domestic sources of influence on U.S. foreign policy, and give examples of each.

34. Consider the role of public opinion and the media in foreign policy, and discuss the extent to which they should influence foreign policy.

35. Briefly describe the history of foreign policy in the United States, and discuss how and why U.S. foreign policy is likely to change in the future.

36. Explain the circumstances that led the United States to use military forces in Afghanistan and Iraq and how these circumstances changed the way that the U.S. thinks about international relations.

# ANSWER KEY

## Answers to Chapter 1

### Fill in the Blanks
1. Politics
2. legitimate
3. tradition, charisma, legality
4. government
5. representative
6. initiative
7. social contract
8. minority
9. executive, legislative, judicial
10. poverty

### Multiple Choice
11. d
12. c
13. d
14. d
15. a
16. a
17. a
18. c
19. d
20. d
21. b
22. d
23. c
24. b
25. d

### True or False
26. True
27. False
28. True
29. False
30. False

# Answers to Chapter 2

## Fill in the Blanks
1.  English
2.  Articles of Confederation
3.  Shays's Rebellion
4.  Articles of Confederation
5.  Electoral College
6.  Federalists
7.  national
8.  judicial review
9.  popular sovereignty
10. Federalist Papers

## Multiple Choice
11. a
12. a
13. c
14. c
15. b
16. c
17. b
18. d
19. a
20. c
21. c
22. d
23. d
24. a
25. b

## True or False
26. False
27. True
28. False
29. True
30. True

## Answers to Chapter 3

Fill in the Blanks
1. confederation
2. delegated, implied
3. reserved
4. delegated
5. full faith and credit
6. state
7. interstate compacts
8. guarantee
9. block
10. new

Multiple Choice
11. c
12. d
13. d
14. c
15. b
16. d
17. d
18. a
19. b
20. d
21. d
22. d
23. a
24. d
25. b

True or False
26. True
27. True
28. False
29. False
30. False

### Fill in the Blanks
1.   political culture
2.   political socialization
3.   school
4.   sampling
5.   tracking
6.   exit
7.   yellow journalism
8.   muckrakers
9.   sound bite
10.  biased

### Multiple Choice
11.  b
12.  d
13.  a
14.  c
15.  d
16.  b
17.  c
18.  c
19.  a
20.  d
21.  a
22.  c
23.  a
24.  b
25.  d

### True or False
26.  True
27.  False
28.  False
29.  True
30.  False

Fill in the Blanks
1. Democratic
2. two-party
3. institutional
4. Federalists
5. Green
6. independents
7. realignment
8. dealignment
9. economic
10. Corporate

Multiple Choice
11. a
12. d
13. c
14. b
15. b
16. a
17. b
18. d
19. b
20. b
21. c
22. b
23. b
24. a
25. d

True or False
26. False
27. True
28. True
29. True
30. False

# Answers to Chapter 6

## Fill in the Blanks
1.  primary
2.  convention
3.  closed
4.  bandwagon
5.  Republican
6.  soft
7.  National Voter Registration
8.  House
9.  one-party
10. midterm

## Multiple Choice
11. b
12. b
13. a
14. a
15. d
16. a
17. c
18. a
19. b
20. d
21. b
22. c
23. b
24. d
25. c

## True or False
26. True
27. True
28. False
29. False
30. False

# Answers to Chapter 7

## Fill in the Blanks
1. regulate
2. continuing resolutions
3. Senate
4. reapportionment
5. gerrymandering
6. oversight
7. five
8. conference
9. filibuster
10. two-thirds

## Multiple Choice
11. c
12. a
13. d
14. c
15. d
16. a
17. b
18. c
19. a
20. d
21. d
22. b
23. d
24. d
25. c

## True or False
26. False
27. True
28. False
29. True
30. False

Answers to Chapter 8

Fill in the Blanks
1.   II
2.   House
3.   Senate
4.   Andrew Jackson, Bill Clinton
5.   Senate
6.   executive agreement
7.   pocket veto
8.   line item veto
9.   impoundment
10.  Watergate

Multiple Choice
11.  d
12.  a
13.  d
14.  b
15.  c
16.  d
17.  a
18.  b
19.  a
20.  d
21.  a
22.  a
23.  a
24.  b
25.  c

True or False
26.  False
27.  False
28.  True
29.  False
30.  True

Fill in the Blanks
1. line, staff
2. secretary
3. agencies
4. corporations
5. spoils
6. merit
7. chief of staff
8. iron triangle
9. whistleblowers
10. fourth

Multiple Choice
11. a
12. c
13. c
14. b
15. d
16. c
17. d
18. a
19. a
20. c
21. b
22. c
23. a
24. d
25. b

True or False
26. False
27. True
28. True
29. True
30. False

## Fill in the Blanks
1. *stare decisis*
2. statutory
3. administrative
4. dual
5. jurisdiction
6. appointment
7. Congress
8. brief
9. dissenting
10. *certiorari*

## Multiple Choice
11. d
12. c
13. a
14. d
15. d
16. c
17. b
18. d
19. a
20. b
21. b
22. b
23. b
24. c
25. b

## True or False
26. False
27. True
28. True
29. False
30. True

# Answers to Chapter 11

## Fill in the Blanks
1.  establishment
2.  Lemon
3.  fighting
4.  sedition
5.  community
6.  public officials
7.  indictment
8.  Geneva Conventions
9.  *ex post facto*
10. electronic

## Multiple Choice
11. b
12. c
13. a
14. a
15. d
16. b
17. a
18. d
19. c
20. a
21. a
22. b
23. c
24. a
25. a

## True or False
26. False
27. False
28. False
29. True
30. False

## Answers to Chapter 12

Fill in the Blanks
1. Thirteenth
2. education
3. W.E.B. Du Bois
4. *de facto*
5. class-action
6. Nineteenth
7. "informed consent"
8. affirmative action
9. Americans with Disabilities Act
10. result

Multiple Choice
11. a
12. c
13. d
14. b
15. b
16. c
17. c
18. d
19. c
20. c
21. b
22. b
23. a
24. d
25. d

True or False
26. True
27. False
28. True
29. True
30. False

Answers to Chapter 13

Fill in the Blanks
1. pluralism
2. interest groups
3. Symbolic
4. Procedural
5. evaluation
6. legitimation
7. Monetary
8. Federal Reserve Board
9. welfare states
10. incomes

Multiple Choice
11. c
12. d
13. b
14. b
15. b
16. c
17. c
18. d
19. b
20. a
21. d
22. a
23. b
24. c
25. b

True or False
26. True
27. True
28. False
29. False
30. False

Fill in the Blanks
1.	realism
2.	Unilateralism
3.	Monroe Doctrine
4.	realpolitik
5.	hegemon
6.	Mercantilist
7.	North Korea; Iran
8.	political ideas
9.	détente
10.	economic

Multiple Choice
11.	c
12.	b
13.	a
14.	a
15.	a
16.	c
17.	c
18.	d
19.	d
20.	b
21.	d
22.	b
23.	d
24.	c
25.	b

True or False
26.	True
27.	True
28.	False
29.	False
30.	True